Cambridge Elements

Elements in Women Theatre Makers
edited by
Elaine Aston
Lancaster University
Melissa Sihra
Trinity College Dublin

LAUREN GUNDERSON AND FEMINIST THEATRE IN THE TWENTY-FIRST CENTURY

Noelia Hernando-Real
Universidad Autónoma de Madrid

Shaftesbury Road, Cambridge CB2 8EA, United Kingdom

One Liberty Plaza, 20th Floor, New York, NY 10006, USA

477 Williamstown Road, Port Melbourne, VIC 3207, Australia

314–321, 3rd Floor, Plot 3, Splendor Forum, Jasola District Centre, New Delhi – 110025, India

103 Penang Road, #05–06/07, Visioncrest Commercial, Singapore 238467

Cambridge University Press is part of Cambridge University Press & Assessment, a department of the University of Cambridge.

We share the University's mission to contribute to society through the pursuit of education, learning and research at the highest international levels of excellence.

www.cambridge.org
Information on this title: www.cambridge.org/9781009487399

DOI: 10.1017/9781009487351

© Noelia Hernando-Real 2025

This publication is in copyright. Subject to statutory exception and to the provisions of relevant collective licensing agreements, no reproduction of any part may take place without the written permission of Cambridge University Press & Assessment.

When citing this work, please include a reference to the DOI 10.1017/9781009487351

First published 2025

A catalogue record for this publication is available from the British Library

ISBN 978-1-009-48739-9 Hardback
ISBN 978-1-009-48740-5 Paperback
ISSN 2634-2391 (online)
ISSN 2634-2383 (print)

Additional resources for this publication at www.cambridge.org/Hernando-Real.

Cambridge University Press & Assessment has no responsibility for the persistence or accuracy of URLs for external or third-party internet websites referred to in this publication and does not guarantee that any content on such websites is, or will remain, accurate or appropriate.

For EU product safety concerns, contact us at Calle de José Abascal, 56, 1°, 28003 Madrid, Spain, or email eugpsr@cambridge.org

Lauren Gunderson and Feminist Theatre in the Twenty-First Century

Elements in Women Theatre Makers

DOI: 10.1017/9781009487351
First published online: November 2025

Noelia Hernando-Real
Universidad Autónoma de Madrid

Author for correspondence: Noelia Hernando-Real, noelia.hernando@uam.es

> **Abstract:** This Element is the first scholarly study of the theatre of Lauren Gunderson (b. 1982), one of the most produced US playwrights and a self-declared feminist playwright. Her feminist claims and theatrical interventions are assessed through four key strands of her theatre making: parodies of Shakespeare's canon; women-centred revisions to history; women and illness; and 'entertaining' feminism through popular theatre forms. Moving between the mainstream and the experimental, her theatre ranges from realism and quasi well-made plays to the experimental in a postmodern/Brechtian fashion, inviting consideration of the form(s) deployed for staging feminism in the twenty-first century. The Element discusses how Gunderson adapts the legacies of second-wave feminist theatre in the United States to provide accessible experimental theatre and how she adopts popular genres in the interest of popular feminisms, giving way to an 'in-between' feminist practice: a feminist-theatre pathway that lies somewhere 'in between' the second-wave past and new directions.

Keywords: Lauren Gunderson, feminist theatre, popular feminisms, popular entertainment, intersectionality

© Noelia Hernando-Real 2025

ISBNs: 9781009487399 (HB), 9781009487405 (PB), 9781009487351 (OC)
ISSNs: 2634-2391 (online), 2634-2383 (print)

Contents

Introduction: Approaching Lauren Gunderson. Feminist, Playwright, Teacher   1

1 Feminist Parody and the Canon   6

2 Feminist Historiography for Badass Women   22

3 Feminist Approach to the Medical Humanities: On Women and Illness   35

4 Feminist Popular Entertainment   46

    Conclusion   60

    References   63

Introduction: Approaching Lauren Gunderson. Feminist, Playwright, Teacher

Despite Lauren Gunderson (born 1982) being the most produced US playwright in recent years according to the prestigious *American Theatre Magazine* (2014–2015, 2018–2019, 2022–2023), academic attention to her theatre is relatively scant. This Element fills this void by offering the first scholarly study of Gunderson's theatre. A self-declared feminist playwright, Gunderson is a dramatist politically concerned with changing the status of women and others marginalized by a still male-dominated world. Her feminist claims and theatrical interventions are assessed through four key strands of her theatre making: Gunderson's parodies of Shakespeare's canon; women-centred revisions to history; re-presentations of women as agents rather than as objects in Medical Humanities; and 'entertaining' feminism through popular theatre forms. As her theatre moves between the mainstream and the experimental, it ranges from realism and quasi well-made plays to the experimental in a postmodern/Brechtian fashion, inviting consideration of the form(s) deployed for staging feminism in the twenty-first century. In one way, the popular forms and feminisms Gunderson frequently espouses could be seen negatively as rupturing the orthodoxies of feminist theatre-making in the United States. However, by exploring the four key strands of Gunderson's theatre, the argument presented in this Element is that her theatre exemplifies new strategies: adapting the legacies of second-wave feminist theatre in the United States to provide accessible experimental theatre and adopting popular genres in the interest of popular feminisms. Hers is what I will ultimately identify and claim as an 'in-between' feminist practice: a feminist-theatre pathway that lies somewhere 'in between' the second-wave past and new directions. Overall, with its focus primarily on Gunderson, the Element will further and more broadly illuminate the diverse strategies of US feminist theatre in the twenty-first century.

Almost ten years after Lauren Gunderson made her first appearance at the very top of the *American Theatre Magazine* list of the most produced playwrights in America, a position she has retained, the scale and prestige of her output are such that it merits sustained, focused, critical, and scholarly attention. Educated at Emory University, with an MFA in Dramatic Writing at NYU Tisch School of the Arts, where she was also a Reynolds Fellow in Social Entrepreneurship, Gunderson is a two-time winner of the Steinberg/ATCA New Play Award, winner of the Lanford Wilson Award and the Otis Guernsey New Voices Award, a finalist for the Susan Smith Blackburn Prize and John Gassner Award for Playwriting, and a recipient of the Mellon Foundation's Residency with Marin Theatre Company. Her works are commissioned by theatres from all around the United States: the South Coast Repertory Theatre, the Kennedy Center, the SF Playhouse, the McCarter Theatre Center, or the Cincinnati Shakespeare Company, to name a few, and produced worldwide, from NYC's Women Project Theatre and Washington DC's Folger Library, to London West End and Hampstead Theatre, to, more recently, China, the Philippines, and Greece. A prolific writer; her works, including plays and collaborations in musicals, number more than fifty and have started to be widely accessible. While half her production remains in manuscripts or published by the Playscripts Inc. or the Dramatists Play Service, more recently, prestigious publishers such as Samuel French or Methuen Bloomsbury have edited individual plays. Editorial confirmation of Gunderson's burgeoning popularity has recently been validated in the publishing of *Revolutionary Women: A Play Collection by Lauren Gunderson* by Methuen Bloomsbury in 2024, an anthology including five plays, edited by Julie Felise Dubiner.

In one of the few introductions to Gunderson's work to date, Holly L. Derr notes the disparity between critical and audience responses to some of Gunderson's plays (2022: 73). Both prolific and popular, to her credit, during some seasons there have been more than 10 different plays by her produced across the United States, many theatre critics, nevertheless, are negative. Even a superficial analysis of reviews, notably those written for high-impact newspapers such as the *Washington Post* or the *New York Times*, reveals a long-held gendered bias against women playwrights. In the United States, women playwrights continue to suffer from the gender prejudice of male theatre reviewers, who are still in the majority and working for the most prestigious papers. And thus a paradox continues to be sustained. The present is an exciting moment for women in the theatre in the United States, as exemplified by Gunderson herself, Sarah Ruhl, Lynn Nottage, or Quiara Alegria Hudes, among many others. And '[t]heir voices have acquired new strength and momentum that have in turn generated greater awareness about gender equality and ignited small changes toward that elusive goal' (Pipino 2020). Nevertheless, success in the theatre system is mainly encountered by straight white men (Pipino 2020), and mainly because, as Gunderson claims, 'usually older, white, men' determine the "worthiness' or 'success' of a play or production in this country' (in Derr 2022: 81). As Rob Weinert-Kendt has written for *American Theatre*, 'While U.S. theatres have a long way to go in terms of equity, diversity, and inclusion, they are a multicultural utopia compared to the narrow demographics of those who write about the theatre [for professional magazines and journals]' (2017). Gunderson aligns with this standpoint. She denounces that a singular subset of respondents has been allowed to determine the worth of theatre in the States and is confident that more critical perspectives will be supported. In line with recent studies that expand on the ecology of theatre criticism (Dolan 2013, Fricker and MacArthur 2024, Radosavljević 2016, Vaughan 2020), in this Element I give voice to critics and reviewers verbalizing their opinions professionally and non-professionally in both traditional media and digital forms, from well-established journals with international impact to online local newspapers, to personal websites, to theatre companies' YouTube channels, and to blogs. They all are part of Gunderson's audience. And while she has remained determined to 'write for audienc*es*, not an audience of one [i.e., the critic]' (in Derr 2022: 81, emphasis in original), the critical reception of her works and the remarkable absence of critical studies of her work prompt questions about the themes and forms of theatre today in the States. In Derr's words, 'The dismissal of some of Gunderson's theatre by some cultural gatekeepers may indicate a similar hesitancy to treat her self-declared feminist writing seriously today' (2022: 74–75). Contrastingly, the purpose of this Element is to take 'seriously' Gunderson's self-declared feminism and the feminist terrain she argues for her plays.

In interviews, talks, essays, and in her presentation on her Instagram Profile, Gunderson introduces herself as a feminist. Her adoption of the term, which happened after graduation, reveals contemporary anxieties about Feminism and its challenges within a neoliberal context. As Kim Solga has noted, 'Post-feminism is a seductive idea in theory, but it is not (at least, not yet) a reality in practice. [... M]any more women than we might, individually, be able to imagine are still struggling uphill toward the kind of privileges a minority of us enjoy' (2016). As a young woman, Gunderson, feeling privileged, also thought that she did not need Feminism. It was later, she says, 'that I realized I am a capital F Feminist' (2020b). Theatre, indeed, became the means to such realization: 'I think my career has been that co-journey of finding my voice and finding my feminism' (in Derr 2022: 77). And such findings coalesce in what she considers her 'mission': to 'break down that patriarchy' through her theatre (in Derr 2022: 82). Starting with practical notions, Gunderson's playwriting fights patriarchy by providing opportunities for women and feminists regardless of gender. With few exceptions, mostly happening at the beginning of her career, Gunderson writes roles for women. The plays are mostly populated by women; sometimes male roles are altogether absent or designed to be performed by actresses. Furthermore, she insists on, or suggests, having female directors, designers, and stage managers. She is aware that, due to her popularity, her works tend to draw women artists and feminists, something she celebrates and is eager to continue promoting as part of her feminist agenda (in Pipino 2020). As regards the stories she tells, she writes those she rarely gets to otherwise see at the theatre. 'I began writing because I wanted women and girls at the center of every story . . . I wrote the heroes I needed, because I needed them to embody and inspire people like me' (2024c: viii). Her focus becomes women and the notion of sisterhood, concerns that vividly remind us of feminist theatre in the wake of the 1980s second wave (Canning 1996: 15) and are present in the works of feminist playwrights who have challenged and inspired her: Caryl Churchill, Maria Irene Fornés, Marsha Norman, Tina Howe, and Lorraine Hansberry (2024c: vii). Gunderson chooses these stories not just because they have been ignored, but because they are valuable and necessary. In her own words: 'I don't want to tell stories of women just because they are true, or because I should. I want to tell them because I think they are better stories – better because these heroes are doubly tested by bias, dis-invitation, and outright denial ... Just on pure dramatic potential, those stories are far richer in struggle and thus far greater in triumph' (2024a: 507). Benefitting from second-wave feminism, but chronologically rooted in the third wave, Gunderson's plays, as I will argue, expose the challenges of present-day feminism and feminist theatre in the United States. Her theatre is heir to US 1970s–1980s feminist practice, informed by that contemporary second-wave feminism, as she provides continuity to the project of voicing women's unheard stories, foregrounding women's subjectivity, at the same time that she destabilizes the patriarchal male gaze. On the one hand, her race and class privilege have helped her to garner public approval; she often writes about white, heterosexual, well-educated women, which accounts for her popularity with this audience demographic. On the other, the variety of women she depicts, the notes on casting across race, sex and gender she frequently calls for, and the specific themes she chooses for her plays also invite consideration of the possible intersectional feminist impetus and impact of her plays.

In her conception of her art, Gunderson has noted that theatre for her is a means to analyse society: 'We are not a mirror, we are a lens. We see what's coming, we embody it, we catalyse it, and we make the better future happen because we tell its story first' (2013). Departing from Aristotelian notions of mimesis or a Brechtian conceptualization of theatre as a hammer with which to shape society, Gunderson's approach is feminist in a way that recalls Jill Dolan's feminist criticism. In Dolan's words, feminism 'provides a way of looking at the world, *a lens* through which to consider how power circulates around the axis of not just gender, but of sexuality, race, and class. Feminism is an analytical system that gives tools for seeing ourselves in relation to one another' (2013: 1, emphasis added). Significantly, a feminist approach to Gunderson's theatre as the one that underlines this Element is also grounded on Dolan's theory that feminism 'offers a transformative politics of hope so that we can imagine, together, a better, more equitable future for us all' (2013: 1).

In general terms, the analysis of Gunderson's plays through a cultural materialist lens which prioritizes subject matter and intention reveals their feminist spirit. The case of Gunderson's formal choices, nevertheless, is not so clear cut. Some of her plays are clearly experimental, but in most of her works, Gunderson seems to prioritize an emotional realist model, largely seen as antithetical to US feminist theatre. Feminist critical strategies in use in the 1970s and 1980s gave way to a dichotomic generic distinction as to what is feminist and what is not that is still difficult to overcome. For second-wave feminist critics, feminist playwrights had to resist stage realism, the form used by patriarchy, they claimed, to perpetuate the status quo and thus women's subjugation (see Case 1988 and Solga 2016). Gunderson joins a significant number of feminists who have written acclaimed realist works, such as Paula Vogel, Lynn Nottage or Wendy Wasserstein, and makes evident the heterogeneity of the genre well into the twenty-first century. As Elaine Aston has said as regards contemporary British women playwrights' use of realism, applications of realism are fluid and 'reflect a shift away from those conservatively formed, phallocentric uses of the genre that were previously the object of feminist criticism, opening up realist conventions to humancentric ends' (2016: 32). However, to Gunderson's use of realism, there is another problematic layer as regards feminism: her use of emotions. Sentimentality seems to be detached from feminist politicizing possibilities, an argument that Aston has pioneered in questioning (2013a: 23). This Element will argue that the overt exploitation of emotions is inherent to Gunderson's updated second-wave motto 'The Personal is Political', which in her dramaturgy reads, 'The Personal is Powerful' and translates into strategies to provoke empathy that will lead to political action. When Gunderson turns to emotional realism, she employs it as a tool rather than an orthodox monolith, using it to strengthen her storytelling while deconstructing realism from within. One of Gunderson's stylistic trademarks, even in her most realistic and well-made works, is to include a moment of transformation, sometimes Brechtian in an alienating fashion, a dismantling of realistic storytelling reminiscent of Elin Diamond's Gestic theory that Gunderson uses to expose the ideology of gender and throw it back at spectators (1997: 46). And yet, Diamond's Gestic theory does not fully apply to Gunderson's work, but then neither can her theatre be understood as conforming to a purely realist/emotional model. Gunderson's theatre as an 'in-between' practice poses the question to be explored in the Element of what value this has for contemporary feminist theatre and feminist concerns. All in all, with this Element I propose a reading of Gunderson's plays from the spirit of Jill Dolan's 'feminist spectator in action'. With Dolan and Gunderson, I see both theatre and feminism as a lens through which to consider the status of women and to work towards a more equitable future for all. The examination of Gunderson's works from a feminist optics will help me confirm what seems obvious at first sight, that is, her status as a feminist playwright, but furthermore, this analysis will help me answer some other questions, such as: What can we glean from analysing the way Gunderson works and collaborates to nurture more feminist drama? What can we learn from reading/seeing her most significant plays from a feminist perspective? And overall, what does her theatre model or exemplify for contemporary feminism and feminist theatre in the United States?

1 Feminist Parody and the Canon

In their zeal to question cultural representations of women in the Western world, second-wave feminist scholars started protesting the systematized neglect of women's experiences in the literary canon. As they argued, the predominantly male authors in the canon either ignored women or misrepresented them in their work, very frequently also showing 'us the female character and relations between the sexes in a way that both reflects and contributes to sexist ideology' (Robinson 1983: 84). These scholars' questioning of such canon took different paths. In the United States Annette Kolodny, with *The Lay of the Land* (1975), and Judith Fetterley, with *The Resisting Reader* (1978), provided alternative readings to the canon, arguing that male writers' notion of universality comes in terms that are purely male. Another significant segment of feminist criticism in the field of literature focused on the study of women writers, in which case two distinct positions as regards the canon are identified. On the one hand, feminist efforts resulted in the humanization of the canon by incorporating works by women into the established canon. Following a case-by-case strategy, the protest against the denial of some women writers' value, when this had once been recognized, resulted in their restoration to the first rank of approval. Such are the cases of Mary Shelley, Jane Austen, Edith Wharton, or Louisa May Alcott. On the other hand, and related to this case-by-case strategy, feminist critics, such as Sandra M. Gilbert and Susan Gubar (1979, 2021) or Elaine Showalter (1977), aimed to dismantle the isolation of these key figures by arguing a female tradition, a female canon in itself, distinct and at times tangential to that other established canon. Such a counter-canon, so to speak, judges the worth of women writers' works by their resistance to male writers' values, both aesthetic and thematic, resulting in the opening of possibilities.

Second-wave feminist scholars' contestation as regards the theatrical and dramatic canon was a more strenuous task from the start. Theatre, in its historical association with the public sphere, lack of decorum and even sin, had traditionally sidelined women, denying their role as playwrights, actresses, directors, designers or in stage management. In the United States, the bastard art, to borrow Susan Harris Smith's definition (1997), was left on the margins of the academic canonical debate. As with the more general literature canon, the revision of the dramatic canon relied heavily on the re-reading of works by male playwrights, most notably those by William Shakespeare. Juliet Dusinberre's *Shakespeare and the Nature of Women* (1975), Lenz, Greene and Neely's *The Woman's Part: Feminist Criticism of Shakespeare* (1980), and Irene G. Dash's *Wooing, Wedding, and Power: Women in Shakespeare's Plays* (1981) illustrate such a feminist critical perspective. The need for the recovery of women's roles in the theatre is evident in volumes such as Chinoy and Jenkins' *Women in American Theatre* (1987), *Notable Women in American Theatre* (1989), edited by Alice M. Robinson, Vera Mowray Roberts, and Milly S. Barran, or Julie Holledge's *Innocent Flowers: Women in the Edwardian Theatre* (1981), and this is a task that continues to be performed in the twenty-first century, as proven by works such as the recent *Routledge Anthology of Women's Theatre, Theory, and Dramatic Criticism* (2024), edited by Catherine Burroughs and J. Ellen Gainor, or Natasha Korda's *Women's Work and the Early Modern English Stage* (2011). Attempts to restore women playwrights to accepted positions in the canon were apparent in their inclusion in authoritative anthologies, such as Gilbert and Gubar's *Norton Anthology of Literature by Women* (1985), which, however, only includes four plays by women (a fact that underlines the marginalization of theatre also in early reformulations of the canon), and in the later *Norton Anthology of Drama* (2009), edited by J. Ellen Gainor, Stanton B. Garner, Jr., and Martin Puchner.

Polarized views as regards the value of the canon and feminist scholars' contribution to its very existence have been nowhere more evident than in feminist theatre scholarship. After attacking the male-dominated theatre canon, pioneer and influential feminist critic Sue-Ellen Case did not see in a counter female canon any solution (1988). Meanwhile, other feminist scholars, perhaps foreseeing the survival of the notion of the canon, did contribute to foster such a notion. June Schlueter's *Modern American Drama: The Female Canon* (1991) both recovered lost voices, such as those of Susan Glaspell, Rachel Crothers, or Sophie Treadwell, and made the case for the value of contemporary voices, such as those of Maria Irene Fornés or Marsha Norman. This latest task, arguing the value and worth of contemporary women playwrights, was replicated in other volumes published in those same years, such as Enoch Brater's *Feminine Focus* (1989) or Lynda Hart's *Making a Spectacle: Feminist Essays on Contemporary Women's Theatre* (1989).

Well into the twenty-first century, women playwrights' relation with the canon remains a site of scholarly debate. The collected essays in Sharon

Friedman's *Feminist Theatrical Revisions of Classic Works: Critical Essays* (2009) provide varied examples of contemporary adaptations of canonical works, from Euripides and Shakespeare to Charlote Brontë or Virginia Wolf. As Friedman argues in the introduction, the revision of the classics, 'often in a subversive mode, has evolved into its own theatrical genre in recent years, and many of these productions have been informed by feminist theory and practice' (2009: 1). In Friedman's, and her collaborators' approach, feminist revisions of the canon arise from the intersection of experimental theatre, traditional literary adaptation, and feminist theatre theory, revisions parallel to feminist scholars' exploration of ingrained notions of gender in canonical texts. In Friedman's words: 'As feminist critics began to use historicist, psychoanalytic, and deconstructive approaches to probe constructions of gender absorbed and interpreted by dramatic works, playwrights and directors – working in this cultural milieu – have experimented with dramatic form, mise-en-scène, language, and the body to foreground and re-present images of women and gender ideology woven into canonical texts, established genres, and theater practices' (2009: 1). Throughout the collection the notion of dialogue brings together canonical texts and their adaptations, theatrical dialogues that aim to mediate between the source texts and their contemporary revisions. In Friedman's view, the analyses of contemporary adaptations, which necessarily consider the historical context, cultural ideology, and theatrical and dramatic nuances, leave the source texts 'intact' (2009:1). While Friedman's affirmation refers to the preservation of the source texts, insisting that the revisions are presented as 'transformations of the classic text' (2009: 14), it reveals contemporary anxieties as regards the status of canonical texts and the dialogues one may establish to get the audience's approval.

Lauren Gunderson has been raised in a culture of veneration of canonical texts. As she has admitted, she was taught – and forced to believe – that canonical texts by male authors set the standards of literary excellence and were universal (2024b). As a young student, she struggled to agree with such prescriptions:

> Most of my young life in Decatur, GA, I absorbed that the characters capable of those great stories were men: Hamlet, Willy Loman, Tom in *The Glass Menagerie*. The women were always on the sidelines, or if they were the main character (Nora for example) they were almost entirely alone in a world of men. This I couldn't stand. (2024c: vii)

As a mature writer now, she also laments the gender bias that has manipulated the canon, wondering 'how much more rich [*sic*] the canon of literature would have been if there'd been more plays where women actually got to talk about what really is important to them and show their lives in progress' (2020c). Her playwrighting has become her way of giving women whole great stories, the means through which she hopes she might 'amplify, add to, and perhaps even join the canon of feminist playwrights' that include, in her own listing, Paula Vogel, Sarah Ruhl, Lynn Nottage, Caryl Churchill, Maria Irene Fornés, Marsha Norman, Tina Howe, Sarah Kane and Lorraine Hansberry (2024c: vii). What brings such a varied group of transatlantic writers to Gunderson's female canon is that they challenge the established canon as they 'speak to and for me' (2024c: vii).

Gunderson's aspirations to be part of this female theatre canon partake in ongoing revisions of the male canon. A very substantial part of her *oeuvre* revisits in different ways and to different extents canonical works by men, the bottom line being giving voice to women. For example, Wendy becomes the protagonist in her revision of J. M. Barrie's classic *Peter Pan*, now consistently entitled *Peter Pan and Wendy*,[1] and written 'with a modern, feminist, indigenous American lens' (2020e). As Celia Wren, writing for the *Washington Post* notes, Gunderson transforms Barrie's story of boyhood into manhood, into one that includes aspects of 'girlhood, womanhood, feminism and "the courage of feeling"'. And, in contrast to Peter Pan's original comrade Wendy Darling, traditionally 'portrayed as mother to the Lost Boys and rival to a jealous Tinker Bell', Gunderson makes of her a 'fledgling scientist' whose role model is Barrie's contemporary Marie Curie (Wren 2019). Sexism is not the only wrong Gunderson was determined to set right in this version. Originally appalled by the racism in the original text, she decided to counter it. While some other contemporary versions of *Peter Pan* have chosen to just eliminate the racist oversimplification of Native American cultures, with hers, Gunderson tries to 'create something that indigenous communities can feel respected by and hopefully encouraging of' (in Hertvik 2019). Openly acknowledging that, as a white woman, she did not know much about the experience, she sought indigenous consultants, including Isabella Star LaBlanc, the actress portraying Tiger Lily at the world premiere at Shakespeare Theatre Company (Hertvik 2019). In LaBlanc's words, she was thrilled 'Tiger Lily gets to be powerful and reclaim her agency and her voice' (in Brady 2020). Judging by reviews, Gunderson's new *Peter Pan and Wendy* is an entertaining revision of Barrie's work that maintains the magic but denounces colonialism from a feminist

---

[1] Barrie first wrote the play *Peter Pan, or The Boy Who Wouldn't Grow Up*, which premiered in London in 1904. The novel version, published in 1911, was titled *Peter Pan and Wendy*, although later editions have always shortened it to *Peter Pan*. Gunderson's recovery of the original title subscribes the protagonism she gives to Wendy, in tune with Jessica Nelson's recent re-edition of Barrie's novel and Disney's 2023 film *Peter Pan & Wendy*, directed by David Lowery.

perspective, without being preachy or lecturing her audience (Brady 2020, Glyer 2019). Gunderson has also revisited the work of Samuel Beckett, whose aging Krapp inspired her female character afflicted with cancer in her ten-minute play entitled *Last Tape*, explored in Section 3 of this Element. Gunderson has also joined the number of female playwrights who have identified and adapted the feminist potential of Euripides' *The Trojan Women*, such as Ellen McLaughlin (2011) or Caroline Bird (2012) with their respective plays under the same title. Unlike these two plays, which exploit the aftermath of the Trojan war as the setting for women's subsequent victimization, Gunderson brings Euripides' characters to '*One room in a little house somewhere near where you live*' (2020: 2) to denounce sex trafficking worldwide regardless of war settings. The play's original title, 'Trojan Women ATL', calls for the replacement of the last word with the abbreviations of the airports where the play is produced, which, together with the setting and present-day speech, reminds audiences of the ubiquity of this problem. The play, summarized as 'Four women, caught, captured, victims with no way out. But this is not ancient Greece. This is your city right now. And this is not going to be a tragedy' was a finalist for the 2023 L. Arnold Weissberger New Play Award, celebrating unpublished, exceptional new plays.

The bulk of Gunderson's plays which revisit the male canon deals with the playwright who has been considered 'the centre of the embryo of a world canon' (Bloom 1994: 59), that is, with William Shakespeare and his work. In a talk about her relationship with Shakespeare, Gunderson admits her endeavour to comprehend his universality and greatness, values of the English playwright ingrained in our cultural memory. And while she affirms that she has learned the craft of drama from Shakespeare, above all as regards 'those deeply universal emotional cliffs' in which he places his characters, she maintains a double-edged relationship with him (2024b).

This relation with Shakespeare is at the core of her ongoing Shakespeare cycle, a collection of eight plays, to the present, in which she revisits the world of Shakespeare. This is a task she finds 'fulfilling and exciting' (2024b) and which reveals the playwright's varied positions as regards Shakespeare. Celebratory in some cases, while deeply challenging in others, the analysis of Gunderson's Shakespeare cycle is enlightening as regards contemporary women playwrights' relation with Shakespeare and the revision of his works for feminist purposes in the twenty-first century. Gunderson's nuanced position is concomitant with worldwide female practices around the figure of Shakespeare, chosen as 'a fellow traveler toward equity and social justice'. In Solga's words, these artists combine their personal interests in everything 'he' might be with a strong political awareness of how the very idea of Shakespeare has always been organized and gate-kept for the benefit of some and at the expense of others. Their love is necessarily dissonant, and their artistic processes – intersectional; cosmologically Indigenous; decentralized and non-hierarchical; committed to resource-sharing and mentorship – proudly foreground that dissonance as an equity-seeking move. (2024: 6)

Gunderson's Shakespeare cycle takes its place within a continuum of theatrical practice and scholarship that expand political ownership over Shakespeare beyond a white male (British) perspective.[2] The plays themselves, together with her collaborative nature and her call for inclusive casting, constitute her feminist contribution to building a more equal world, also via Shakespeare.

Gunderson's upfront celebration of Shakespeare and his meaning to theatre and drama history is most evident in *The Book of Will* (2016), commissioned by the Denver Centre Theatre Company and winner of the Harold and Mimi Steinberg/American Theatre Critics Association New Play Award in 2018. The play is a historical drama, where many liberties are taken, that tells of Shakespeare's friends' efforts to put his plays together posthumously in what came to be known as Shakespeare's First Folio (1623). His influence throughout history is evident in a very theatrical ending that celebrates his *oeuvre* when lines from his plays are read and displayed on stage in different languages, an ending that critics have found 'powerful' (Velasco 2018) and a 'culmination' (Harris 2023). But beyond celebratory impulses, Gunderson uses the story of Henry Condell and John Heminges to underline how fellowship and family preserved Shakespeare's works. While the play has not gone too 'deep' in history, as David Jays laments in the *Guardian*, it does succeed as 'an affecting

---

[2] Scholars have been examining Shakespeare's relation to patriarchy, gender, race, white supremacy, colonialism, and postcolonialism for several decades. Titles include *The Woman's Part: Feminist Criticism of Shakespeare* (1980), edited by Carolyn Ruth Swift Lenz, Gayle Greene, and Carol Thomas Neely, Dympna Callaghan's *Shakespeare Without Women* (1999), Carol Chillington Rutter's *Enter the Body: Women and Representation on Shakespeare's Stage* (2001), Kim F. Hall's *Things of Darkness* (1996), Ania Loomba and Martin Orkin's *Post-colonial Shakespeares* (1998), *The Cambridge Companion to Shakespeare and Race* (2021), edited by Ayanna Thompson, Arthur L. Little, Jr's *White People in Shakespeare* (2022); and Farah Karim-Cooper's *The Great White Bard* (2023), to name a few. On this line, the wealth of theatre practitioners revisiting Shakespeare and his world for the stage is overwhelming. Examples of plays include Ann-Marie MacDonald's *Good night Desdemona (Good morning Juliet)* (1990), Paula Vogel's *Desdemona* (1993), Marina Carr's *Portia Coughlan* (1996), and Winsome Pinnock's *Rockets and Blue Lights* (2021). Remarkable intersectional interventions in the direction of institutions devoted to staging and/or studying Shakespeare include Emma Rice's leadership of Shakespeare's Globe and Farah Karim-Cooper's recent appointment as director of the Folger Shakespeare Library. Last but not least, in *Women Making Shakespeare in the Twenty-First Century* (2024), Kim Solga explores the processes of transformation of Shakespeare's plays, known to be patriarchy-affirming, ableist, and often racist, into vehicles towards equity at the hand of women creators around the globe.

play about friendship's ardent joys and responsibilities' (2023). Gunderson's aim with the play was, after all, making Shakespeare more human:

> And I think that's part of what I loved in telling this story, too, is we have such reverence for Shakespeare as we should. But to them [Heminges and Condell], he was their best friend. He was of course a great talent and a great voice of that era but he was also Will, the guy that they saw flirt with the wrong people and get too drunk and, you know, mess up his lines, because of course he was human. And that's really when I realized that this story can be not just for the Shakespeare nerds among us or the historians, but for everybody. Because I think Shakespeare doesn't need that much help in being revered. He needs help in being human. That's the real heart of this story. (Gunderson 2017)

Thus, in Gunderson's story of fellowship and Shakespeare's humanization for the common people, women are given fundamental roles. The characters of Rebecca and Alice, John Heminges' wife and daughter respectively, complete and balance the man, as does Elizabeth Condell with respect to her husband. The three women are also seen onstage reading and reviewing the scripts, perhaps an imagined scene that visualizes, nonetheless, these women's support of their men and, consequently, their role in making Shakespeare's legacy last. The appearance of Anne Hathaway Shakespeare towards the end of the play, when Heminges and Condell show her the manuscript, a scene that might have happened, is meant to confront that 'strange academic animosity' to her. Gunderson's Anne is strong and loving, a widow who understands the great work that had kept her husband apart from the family and made of her a *de facto* single mother. As Gunderson has said about the female characters in this play, 'there are a few but I really wanted to make sure that this play has enough women in the way that Shakespeare's plays themselves are populated with really interesting, compelling, ambitious, powerful, funny women' (Gunderson 2017). *The Book of Will* is the only play in Gunderson's Shakespeare's cycle anchored in the format of historical drama. The other seven plays, written in different genres and showing different attitudes towards Shakespeare's works, all share a concern with *The Book of Will*: bringing to the stage strong, independent, and full-voiced women.

Lauren Gunderson's strategy to revisit Shakespeare's works is that of parody, a term widely used in Postmodernity and which requires clarification. As Linda Hutcheon, one of the main theorists on parody, has said: 'Parody is a complex genre, in terms of both its form and its ethos. It is one of the ways in which modern artists have managed to come to terms with the weight of the past. The search for novelty in twentieth-century art has often – ironically – been firmly based in the search for a tradition' (2000: 29). According to Margaret Rose, historically there have been two positions as regards parody: either mocking, that is, showing contempt for the original material, or sympathetic, that is, conveying admiration for the imitated text (1979). Departing from notions of mere imitation and the sought after effect of laughter identified by Rose and others in parody, Linda Hutcheon finds two impulses in contemporary parody that help categorization: conservative or subversive impulses. In Hutcheon's words,

> The presupposition of both a law and its transgression bifurcates the impulse of parody: it can be normative and conservative, or it can be provocative and revolutionary. Its potentially conservative impulse can be seen in both extremes of the range of ethos, reverence and mockery: parody can suggest a 'complicity with high culture ... which is merely a deceptively off-hand way of showing a profound respect for classical-national values' (Barthes 1972: 119), or it can appear as a parasitical form, mocking novelty in the hope of precipitating its destruction (and, by implication, its own). Yet parody can, like the carnival, also challenge norms in order to renovate, to renew. (2000: 76)

The later kind of parody, aiming to be revisionary and revolutionary, is the one Gilbert and Gubar already identified in much female writing from the nineteenth century (1979: 80), a female tradition in which Lauren Gunderson participates. Borrowing Hutcheon's words on the possibilities of parody, with her Shakespeare's plays, Gunderson is coming to terms 'with formal literary conventions and with the past', constituting simultaneously an 'act of emancipation'. Her use of parody is an empowering tool as it acts 'to signal distance and control in the encoding act' (2000: 96).

The conception of parody as an empowering tool through agency leads to recent discussions on the distinction between adaptation and appropriation within Shakespeare studies. As Alexa Huang, Elizabeth Rivlin and Douglas Lanier, among others, have discussed, adaptation has come to be seen as the translation of Shakespeare's original texts to different media, a translation based on the respect to what is the 'essence' of the original work. This notion of essence, nonetheless, is problematic, residing sometimes in language, plotting, characters or themes, and other times in the 'accuracy' or 'authenticity', notions problematic as well in themselves (Huang and Ruvlin 2014: 7–8, Lanier 2014: 23–24). While some of Gunderson's works might be said to respect Shakespeare's essence to some extent, as the theme of ambition in *Toil and Trouble* (2012), based on *Macbeth*, or the extensive quotations from *Hamlet* in 'A Room of the Castle' (2023), her revisions of Shakespeare fall into the category of appropriation. Unlike adaptations, appropriations involve clearer overtones of agency and convey political, cultural advocacy. As Christy Desmet has put it, appropriation should be seen 'not just as theft, but as a recursive process of give and take. From this perspective as well, rewritings with artistic and political motivations are no longer opposed to one another, but exist along a continuum governed by the contingencies of their reception' (2014: 43).

Gunderson's process of 'give and take' with Shakespeare responds to such contingencies of reception. On the one hand, as a reader of Shakespeare herself, her rewritings show her own reception of his works. On the other hand, her parodies of Shakespeare are used as a device to further reinforce the collective and ongoing nature of the theatre-going community. As Marvin Carlson has said, 'In order to enjoy a theatrical parody the audience must be essentially composed of a community that shares a common theatrical history of attending the work being parodied', with pleasure arising from the 'shared recognition of the parody's references, in their exaggerated or distorted form' (2001: 39). And in the dialogue in which Gunderson invites her audience to start with Shakespeare's original texts resides her feminist challenge of Shakespeare and of his shaping of the theatrical canon, as regards both thematic and formal concerns.

Gunderson's first play from her Shakespeare cycle serves as prologue to her cultural and political agenda behind her appropriations of Shakespeare. *Exit, Pursued by a Bear* (2011) is inspired in one of the most famous stage directions in Shakespeare. This stage direction announces the death of Antigonous in the claws of a bear in act III of *Winter's Night*, but parallels between *Exit* with *Winter's Tale* end here. Gunderson's feminist revision of Shakespeare shows in one critic's summary of the play as a 'ratatat meta riff on Shakespearean themes of revenge washed through the modern understanding of the psychological horrors of domestic abuse' (Teachman 2017). Gunderson transforms iconic revenge tragedies typical of the Renaissance into what she defines as 'a revenge comedy' in this highly metatheatrical piece where Nan, the abused wife, teaches her abusive husband Kyle a lesson. Taped to a chair and covered in honey, under threats of a bear in the neighbourhood, Kyle is forced to watch the metatheatrical performance of his abusive behaviour towards Nan. Critics have been divided as regards how comic the play is. Most reviewers have found it 'funny' (Hurwitt 2011), 'witty', 'comic' (Farmer 2016), or 'hilarious' (Lefty 2023). The critic for the *Chicago Tribune* is more specific in defining it as an 'amusing piece of nouveau Southern gothic writing' (Jones 2012). But for others it is 'devoid of humor' (Williams 2012), 'flaccid' and 'absent of humor' (Howey 2023). Significantly, for reviewers like this, Gunderson's appropriation of Shakespeare is unacceptable to the point of offensively saying, 'Keep Shakespeare's words out of your damn mouth' (Howey 2023). While this might seem anecdotal, this reviewer's aggressive note confirms how challenging it is for women playwrights today to parody Shakespeare for feminist purposes.

Gunderson's next two appropriations of Shakespeare also make direct references to this playwright in their titles and constitute comedies. The second play in the cycle, *Toil and Trouble* (2013), is 'a black comedy' defined by Gunderson as an 'uber capitalist hipster *Macbeth*'. A trio formed by the murderous couple Matt and Beth, and Adam; a repository of Banquo, MacDuff and some other characters from *Macbeth*, resist recession by planning the taking over of a small country. This modern retelling of ambition and power includes mocking quotations from *Macbeth* and *Hamlet* and ends happily. Reception has been positive, considering the play as 'a goofy Generation Why retelling of *Macbeth*' (*SF Bay Guardian* 2012) and mainly praising its 'excellent balance of intelligent, pointed humor ... and artful use of Shakespeare' (Reyes 2012). *Toil and Trouble* does not render a significant feminist parody. Silly comedy that it is, it does nevertheless include a strong, powerful, and ambitious revisited Lady Macbeth in Beth, one that, however, misunderstands what Feminism is. As Gunderson mockingly has her say: 'Feminism means I get to be evil too!' (2013: 49). Gunderson's current project, 'Sinister', a pop musical retelling the story of the witches from *Macbeth*, constitutes a more feminist parody on the play. Commissioned by the Chicago Shakespeare Theatre, and with music and lyrics by Joriah Kwamé, this musical is a prequel to *Macbeth*. In her libretto, Gunderson has the witches claim the right to tell their story themselves. All in all, and in tune with the principles of second-wave feminism, 'Sinister' is a call for and a celebration of sisterhood and female bonding to fight patriarchy, which, embodied in the only male character in the play, Macbeth, is not only responsible for women's division and subjugation but for the destruction of nature.

Chronologically, the third play in Gunderson's Shakespeare cycle is *The Taming* (2013), titled after *The Taming of the Shrew*. Gunderson takes on one of the most rebellious female characters in Shakespeare's *oeuvre*, Katherina, and brings her to present-day America. Katherine, Miss Georgia, does not only have beauty contest ambitions, but also political ones. To fulfil her political aspirations, Katherine needs to make the polarized political parties in the United States come to agreements, which is the plot drive that allows Gunderson to revisit the state of American democracy and the current situation of politics in her home country. As Gunderson has said about the play in a blog post on Playscripts.com:

> In 2013 I wrote *The Taming*, an all-female political farce for Crowded Fire Theatre, to unpack the deep frustration of a divided and obstructionist

patriarchy to laugh with the painful truth about extremism on both sides, to toy with our country's history and wrestle with its foundational imperfections, and to make manifest a dream of reason and understanding prevailing in America. That feels more necessary now than three years ago. (in American Theatre Editors 2016)

The play invites us to dream of a female president of the United States, and Gunderson's sense of urgency in debunking patriarchal politicians shows in her waiving the licensing fee of the play on Inauguration Day 2017, when Donald Trump became the 45th President. Theatrical activism aside, the play has been found erratic in plot structure (Coddon 2022), including cartoonish characters which bear little resemblance to Shakespeare's (Launer 2022), but still funny and thought-provoking: 'if it doesn't cut very deep, Gunderson's 'Taming' is a laugh riot with some timely food for thought' (Hurwitt 2013).

Three of the plays in which Gunderson revisits Shakespeare are based on *Hamlet*, a well-known revenge tragedy, which Gunderson appropriates very differently in each case. While unpublished and unproduced to date, 'Or Not. A Short Play in the Wake of Hamlet' (2008) deserves mention as a sequel to *Hamlet*. In this short play, Horatio, who can be played by either an actor or an actress according to the manuscript, is questioned right after everybody's death in the source text. This is a political play, set in the present, about the manipulation of truth. Despite Hamlet's begging at the end of Shakespeare's play, Horatio is not allowed to tell her/his story. The authorities' obtuseness and preconceived ideas lead the audience to think that *Hamlet*'s tragedy and the deaths involved might have no consequences at all. A feminist stance is more obvious in 'A Room in the Castle', Gunderson's most recent addition to her Shakespeare's cycle. The play is a co-production of the Folger Shakespeare Library in Washington DC, where it had a reading in 2023, and the Cincinnati Shakespeare Company, which commissioned the work and held its world premiere in March 2025. With this play Gunderson challenges *Hamlet*, questioning who the hero of the play is. While the play enhances and celebrates *Hamlet* and its beauty, 'with reverence and respect', Gunderson questions, 'whose story this should be' (2024b). The genesis of the play dwells in Gunderson's sense of frustration at Ophelia's character, specifically at 'the abuse she suffers, the sudden madness, the untimely death at her own hand', as well as in her reconsideration of the character of Gertrude: 'I began to contemplate what it must be like to look at your son and be so shocked and dismayed by the violence and mayhem he's capable of and think: Did I do this? Is this my fault?' Her interest in the female characters in *Hamlet* led to a longing to have them together in private, giving way to this 'blend of Shakespeare, intergenerational feminism, and women's survival in a violent patriarchy' (in Shakespeare & Beyond 2023). Treating Ophelia and Gertrude as real people, in the sense that they exist outside Shakespeare's play, and with the only presence of one more female character, Ophelia's nurse, Gunderson provides a new angle to *Hamlet*. By cleverly inserting scenes between real scenes of the original play, from which fragments are quoted, Gunderson gives Ophelia and Gertrude their own voices in private spaces where they can speak safely. And in doing so, they emerge as powerful women who subvert patriarchy – and traditional readings of these characters' victimization in *Hamlet* – through their bonding. 'Together they sing, laugh, and argue', and in doing so, they 'create hope in a hopeless situation' (Folliard 2023). In Gunderson's words, 'This play dances and duels with Shakespeare's *Hamlet*, foregrounding the women in the play and re-imagining them with agency, vitality, and radical hearts eager for a new ending' (2025). Formally, the play mixes Shakespeare's language with contemporary slang and references, underlining the need to keep on challenging what Shakespeare and his women characters mean to us in the twenty-first century. As Kaja Dunn, director of 'A Room in the Castle' has highlighted, 'In this current moment, a story about women fighting for liberation, finding autonomy, and helping the next generation thrive feels incredibly urgent and relevant' (in Higgins 2025). Through her dialogue with *Hamlet*, the play makes evident that it is possible to collaborate with and reject Shakespeare and his shaping of the world at the same time. As Gunderson has said, 'Because this play is anything but hopeless and tragic. These women of this play – the characters, the actors, and the women-led creative team – aren't holding a mirror up to nature. We're shattering the glass' (in Higgins 2025).

Gunderson's collaboration with and appropriation of Shakespeare's work for feminist purposes is also the basis of *Natural Shocks* (2018), whose title is taken from Hamlet's famous soliloquy 'To be or not to be'. Angela, the protagonist and only character in the play, identifies with the tragic hero. 'Hamlet is my people,' she says, in Gunderson's clear attempt to make Angela's story as universal as Hamlet's has come to be seen. Formally, Gunderson transforms Hamlet's soliloquy into a monologue, establishing a direct conversation with spectators, who in a Brechtian sense are requested to take action once the show is over. Gunderson was in high school when the Columbine High School massacre, the deadliest mass shooting in the United States till that date, took place. The draft of the play was ready when, on Valentine's Day of 2018, the Parkland massacre happened. Before the play had its world premiere, *Natural Shocks* was produced nationwide on 20 April 2018, that is, on the 19th anniversary of Columbine and just two months after Parkland. As on other occasions, Gunderson waived her royalty fees, and the play was produced or read at 107 theatres in 48 states and Washington DC to raise awareness and funds for charities dedicated to gun violence prevention. Through Angela, Gunderson makes explicit the link between domestic abuse and mass shootings. Citing statistics, the protagonist says, 'domestic abuse victims are five times more likely to die if there are guns in the house . . . And while perpetrators of domestic violence account for only 10 percent of all gun violence, they account for 54 percent of mass shootings' (2019: 28–29). Angela, who is killed onstage by her invisible husband, is 'the warning sign that no one ever saw' (2019: 30). This line erects the abusive husband and future mass killer into that 'canker of nature [that] come[s] in further evil' in *Hamlet* (act 5). The 'natural shocks' Angela repeats again and again throughout the play come to signify the different kinds of abuses she has been victim of, and which will escalate to a mass shooting that may affect anyone:

> After he shoots me in the heart with my own weapon, he will leave me to bleed.
> And he will do what he's planned.
> And he will drive to a place he knows well.
> And he will unpack his weapons.
> And he will fire on a crowd.
> And he doesn't care who is in it.
> And you might be in it. There is a chance it will be you. Roll the dice.
> Because it's chance that we're here right now, isn't it? (2019: 29–20)

Gunderson establishes more parallels between Angela and Hamlet besides their tragic endings. Hamlet has traditionally been regarded as a Malcontent type, a character who through his confiding soliloquies comments on and plots revenge against the corruptions of society. Angela merges as a feminist malcontent who, through her monologue, unpacks a story of abuse and asks the audience to react. '*"See me," she wishes she could say to you. See me*' are the last words of the play (2019: 30). Gunderson has explicitly expressed she wants her audience to compare Angela to 'this great titanic male figure . . . You would buy Hamlet's story, but not hers?' (in Rebell 2018). Like Hamlet, Angela is an unreliable narrator, whose layers of conflicts are revealed bit by bit. And she shares with Hamlet an undecisive nature, that hamartia that precipitates the tragic ending:

> Hamlet again. To go or not to go. Indecision. Inability to act. Me and Hamlet.
>
> I told myself it was because of my mom's china. It would be too loud and heavy to abscond with it at two A.M., and I couldn't leave it . . . He'd smash it. I know he would . . . I couldn't go. (2019: 19–20)
>
> God, I should have left him so long ago. Why didn't I? it was too hard. Bank accounts, mortgages, divorce and lawyers and bills and – Jesus – I just froze. *Why is my life worth less than my mortgage? Get out, get out, get out Angela!*

Figure 1 Liz Sankarsingh in Echo Theatre's *Natural Shocks* (Courtesy photo by Zack Huggins).[3]

> I used to think I deserved it, that's how bad it was, that's how normal it was.
> I deserved whatever bullshit mini rage he cooked up.
> Well I don't deserve it. (2019: 26, emphasis in original, see Figure 1)

Employing monologue as a journey, Angela reveals that her existential dilemma, unlike Hamlet's, does not involve self-slaughter, but the peril of being murdered by her partner and her own lack of action. Her 'undiscovered country' is not the afterlife, but the possibility of a life without her husband. Such possibility, reflective of the situation of many victims of domestic abuse, keeps being postponed by obstacles as the ones Angela mentions, from self-blame to the management of bank accounts and bills. Gunderson further details how Angela compares to Hamlet:

> What she is doing is talking a hell of a lot to change the world, to save her soul, to be her best self, to fix things, to right wrongs. Those are all the things that Hamlet does. He's very thoughtful about it, and she is very thoughtful about it. He's cheeky, and she's cheeky. It's dangerous in Denmark, and it's dangerous being underground for a tornado. … She's a very strategic and practical person. She's a thinker. And Hamlet is too. I love that the way this

---

[3] *Natural Shocks* was produced at Echo Theatre in Dallas (Texas) in 2023. Full credits: Sasha Maya Ada (director), Eric Berg (producer), Kateri M. Cale (managing & artistic director), Claire Boschert (production stage manager), Claire DeVries (scenic designer), Jamie Milligan (lighting designer), Jasmine Woods (costume designer), Lauren Floyd (graphic artist). See Figure 2 for Lauren Floyd's poster design, a crafty revision of Hamlet's iconic skull in the context of Gunderson's tornado.

Figure 2 Poster design for Echo Theatre's *Natural Shocks* (Courtesy of Lauren Floyd).

character appreciates Hamlet is not the way I appreciate it, which is the poetry and the drama. The way she appreciates it is that he's thinking through the hardest thing, but being practical about it. (in Rebell 2018)

Despite these similarities, the main difference is that, after all the thinking, Angela eventually takes action. A rehearsal in front of the audience of how to tell her husband that she is leaving him turns into what has happened before the beginning of the play, when Angela ran down to the basement, locking the door behind her saying she was seeking shelter from a tornado.

The form Gunderson gives to *Natural Shocks* marks a clear departure from the genre of *Hamlet*. As with other of her appropriations already discussed, Gunderson turns the original tragedy into 'a comedy ... until it's not' (2019: 5). For most of the play, Angela appears as a typical stand-up comedian, quite in the American tradition (Paterson 2015), sharing details from her life in humorous ways, including jokes on her job as an insurance agent and on what is presented as a just not fully pleasant relation with her husband. This is part of Gunderson's strategy to parody the Shakespeare canon from a feminist angle. Angela is not just as witty in her remarks as Hamlet is, she is 'zany' (Rebell 2018). According to Gunderson,

> The biomechanics of physically laughing let us relax and realize there are other people in the room who are thinking the same thing we are. It communalizes, and it conjoins. ... And so, a comedy that is about real things lets an audience get closer to those real things than a drama would. Sometimes, a drama can easily be too much, or as an audience, you can know what you're getting into when you start. But a comedy leans you in. (in Rebell 2018)

Comedy, thus, is one of Gunderson's favourite devices, one that brings her audience together and which she uses to draw the audience into the action. Her second favourite device is the inclusion of a twist in the plot, also present in *Natural Shocks*, when Angela reveals there is no tornado, that 'There is only him' (2019: 29), her husband, that destructive force of nature at the other side of the door. Practically all reviews of the play mention this last-minute plot twist. Negative reviews, such as Laura Collins-Hughes' for the *New York Times*, refer to it as a switcheroo, deus ex machina (2018). Positive reviews, above all coming from common theatre-goers, underline the potential of this device to surprise, shock, and make the show more powerful (Southbank Theatre 2022, 'Speak Up Speak Out' 2018). These spectators' references to their own feelings at the end of the show are in tune with Gunderson's conception of her feminist theatre, one that appeals to emotions to foster change. 'Empathy is one of theatre's superpowers' (Gunderson in Derr 2022: 78).

As seen, Gunderson's parodies, especially those on Shakespeare's works, provide revisions that bring women centre stage, locating them in safe spaces where they can speak their minds. Gunderson's Shakespeare plays reveal some feminist potential in a celebration of Shakespeare's legacy that, at the same time, challenges his portrait of silenced and many times powerless female characters. Critical reception of these plays reveals some reluctance as regards feminist revisions of Shakespeare's themes and genres, reluctance that the general public, accounting for the popularity of these plays, nevertheless, does not seem to share.

2 Feminist Historiography for Badass Women

Feminist historians of the second wave identified a gender gap in dominant historical discourse. The discipline of history and its writing had largely been dictated by white men that objectified, ignored, silenced, and/or misunderstood women. One of the most evident endeavours of feminist historians from the 1970s onwards has been to 'recover the silenced histories of women' (Kelly 2010: 645). Finding these remarkable women from the past would help in providing present-day women with predecessors, with torchbearers who would light the way in the writing of women's history. The notion of Herstory, made popular in the early 1970s, invited women to rewrite history from a feminist lens, making visible women's roles. Volumes such as June Sochen's *Herstory: A Woman's View of American History* (1974) or Nancy Cott's *Roots of Bitterness* (1972) bear witness to this endeavour. Such revisions of history, nevertheless, seem paradoxical, especially in the United States. Referring to such paradox, Charlotte Canning has stated that for second-wave US feminists,

> A disavowal of history released them from being inhibited by the past's oppressive and discriminatory traditions and allowed them to create new forms of knowledge and new practices emerging out of women's experiences. The paradox within this antagonism was that feminism also turned to the very past it was rejecting for precedent and inspiration. Feminists wanted to create everything anew but they also wanted to demonstrate that these creations had legitimacy by justifying them through appeals to the past. (2004: 228)

This simultaneous embracing and troubling of history has informed feminist historiography, so that 'revised histories do not substitute one kind of blindness for another' (Kelly 2010: 645–646). Feminist scholars have identified the danger for feminist hopes of a more equalitarian world in revisions of history tailored to merely 'prove' women's superiority to men or their alleged equality in the past in simplistic celebratory ways (Canning 2004: 230). A more effective approach, some say, does not stop in unearthing and telling the great deeds of women in the past, but exposes 'the silent and hidden operations of gender [... and t]hrough this approach women's history critically confronts the politics of existing histories and inevitably begins the rewriting of history' (Scott 1988: 27).

Parallel to the beginnings of feminist historiography in the mid-1970s, the feminist history play was born on both sides of the Atlantic. Paradigmatic feminist playwrights, such as Caryl Churchill, with *Vinegar Tom* (1976), or Maria Irene Fornés, with *Evelyn Brown* (1980), contributed to a genre that remains alive nowadays. Plays such as Sarah Ruhl's *In the Next Room* (2009) or Deirdre Kinahan's *Wild Notes* (2023) insist on the need to keep revising history and its methodologies. In general terms, feminist history plays invite us to look behind the official version of how events have been said to happen in the past, to reconsider how our cultural memories have collected them. The feminist history play avoids the replication of history writing, the putting together of records to try to comprehend what 'truly' happened. In performance, it should be foregrounded that 'history is not the past but a narrative about the past, one that comes to stand in for that past' (Canning 2004: 231). In this narrative, what the feminist playwright aims to make evident is that gender, sexual orientation, class, and ethnicity are significant and actual historical categories of human identity and experience (Kelly 2010: 660) and, in contrast to traditional history, to question the experiences of white straight men as normative.

The long association of history with the notion of 'reality' has led to the assumption that realism must be the favourite style adopted by history plays. But the relation between feminism and realism, as seen in the Introduction, has been as double-edged as that between feminism and history. Thus, many playwrights favour realism or a combination of realism with minor disruptive forms, commonly towards the end of the plays, as is the case of Ruhl's *In the Next Room*, while others embrace experimentation openly, opting for unconventional 'forms of language, setting, character, and narrative to defamiliarize audience expectations of the performed event' (Kelly 2010: 660), as, for example, Suzan-Lori Parks does in *Father Comes Home from the Wars* (2015). Feminist revisions of history for the stage are also varied in format, from docudramas to the dramatization of overlooked events from the past, to the imagining of ignored events. The bottom line of such plays is the concomitance of past and present and, at their best, the embodiment of the impossibility to provide feminist versions of history as firmly closed as those male-dominated notions of history that feminism aims to dismantle.

Lauren Gundeson's approach to history through her feminist lens somehow echoes both concerns, though the analysis of particular plays reveals nuances in her embrace of these principles. History plays conform a very substantial part of her *oeuvre* as this is a genre that allows her to treat one of her main concerns as a feminist dramatist: the past. In defining her feminist writing, Gunderson has noted that her plays lack personified antagonists, replaced by a set of 'twin antagonists', which are patriarchy and time:

> Both are ever present, both uncompromising, both a threat to everything my characters need, want and strive for. Sexism needs no introduction and needs no walking-talking villain to show up and give our characters the struggle of a lifetime. Time is the universal antagonist ceaselessly challenging my ambitious protagonists to do enough, be enough, love enough, prove enough, know enough before their last breaths. I don't write villains because I don't need to. For my characters the world as it is proves enough of an antagonist. (2024c: viii)

In her history plays, then, Gunderson takes a feminist materialist approach, one that shows historical time, controlled and recorded by patriarchy, to be women's enemy. Her 'bringing history to light through the lens of today' has earned her the appellation 'queen of modern period pieces' (Cohen 2023). As part of her creative process, Gunderson takes research very earnestly, but her creative licences are very evident too. She challenges historic representations of women in the past through imaginary revisions, theatrically mediating in the interpreting of history. As she has said, her history plays are 'mostly true', admitting the writing of scenes that might be 'historically inaccurate', but which are 'true to the feeling' and fundamental for her feminist goal in revising historical events (2020e). Such a position is on the verge of truthiness and overtly prioritizes her own feelings. While valid for her upfront honesty, considering the position from which she writes – that of a white, middle-class US young woman – this statement should raise some scepticism and is not always unproblematic, as following analyses will show.

The imbrication of artistic licences in the writing of history plays is not new to women's theatre. In his historiographical analysis of Suzan-Lori Parks' plays, Harry J. Elam, Jr. has noted that 'the process of history can be one of imaginative creation; that history is not simply found but made, and in the process "Making some [history] up" does not infer that theatre can itself constitute "real" history; rather, it recognizes the unique relationship of the theatre to the "real" as well as the power and value of this creative process of representation' (Elam 2010: 288). As a playmaker, Gunderson also makes some history up, and for her, the power and value of mediating in patriarchal versions of history dwell in imagining other possibilities which, as seen, are 'true to the feeling'. Such an affirmation reveals that Gunderson's role as theatrical archaeologist brings her close to what historians had done from at least the fifth century BCE: intertwining empathy and narrative in historical inquiry (McConacchie 2020: 378). The method of imaginative re-enactment has been widely used by historians, who can only explain and narrate motives behind historical facts by getting inside the mentalities of protagonists of historical situations. Artistic licences seem to also have been integral to a discipline some claimed aims to present facts objectively. However, the tensions about the validity of this method, with R. G. Collingwood as its most ardent advocate, started in the 1940s and remain today (McConachie 2020: 378–379). Matters such as the extent to which historians can make use of their imagination when lacking solid evidence for historical assertions, the thin line between empathy or sympathy, and more boldly, who is entitled to imaginatively re-enact the thoughts of certain people, for example, of people of colour or of previously colonized people, underline present discussions and find echoes in the field of theatre criticism (Shepherd-Barr 2006: 189). With just one exception, to be discussed later, Gunderson revisits the history of white Western women, probably the same demographic of her main audience and to which she also belongs, avoiding claims of misappropriation. Her revisions, as any versions of history, appear as one version of a part of history, one that provides insight into the female mind against a patriarchal context. Through her history plays, Gunderson invites us to understand her female protagonists, to make us 'feel with them' and sense the burden of their historical time, out of which they emerge as heroines. And in the process, she foregrounds the pressures of identity categories of gender and class, and to some extent those of sexual orientation and ethnicity, and invites us to rethink historiography.

Within the genre of history plays, Gunderson has devoted much of her work to writing plays on the history of science. Science, as theatre itself, has been a field dominated by men and reluctant to admit women's contributions. Following the path of second-wave feminist historians, Gunderson has enriched Herstory by writing about female scientists from a feminist perspective. Astronomer Henrietta Leavitt, whose work at the Harvard Observatory in the early 1900s made it possible to measure the universe for the first time in human history, is the protagonist in *Silent Sky* (2013). In *Ada and the Engine* (2015), Gunderson brings centre stage mathematician Ada Lovelace Byron, considered the first computer programmer. And in *The Half-Life of Marie Curie* (2019), Gunderson stages the relation between physicist and chemist Marie Curie, twice winner of a Nobel Prize (for Physics in 1903 and for Chemistry in 1911), and electromechanical engineer Hertha Ayrton. These three plays share a number of features that characterize this strand of Gunderson's approach to history. The three of them are didactic, making science understandable and palatable for general audiences. In the case of *Silent Sky*, the audience witnesses how Leavitt's hard work cataloguing the position and luminosity of stars gives way to discovering the period–luminosity relationship for Cepheid variables. In *Ada and the Engine*, together with Charles Babbage, we see Ada Lovelace imagining a thinking engine, Babbage's Analytical Engine, which not only makes complicated calculations, but also talks to itself, predicts outcomes, and even creates music. *The Half Life of Marie Curie* opens with two odes. In 'Hertha's ode to the electric arc', the character of Hertha Ayrton explains directly to the audience this principle by using an electric lamp. In 'Marie's ode to the radium in her pocket', it is the turn of Marie Curie to tell the audience the process of radiation while holding a piece of radium. These women's extraordinary discoveries, the practical uses of which for the present world are also shown on the stage, are even more extraordinary as they are made within hostile patriarchal environments. Gunderson is direct in denouncing institutionalized sexism. Henrietta is not allowed to use the telescope, the Great Refractor, because she is a woman, one working within George 'Pickering's harem' (2013: 15). Ada needs to accomplish her female duty first, that is, getting married, having children, and proving a good mother and wife, before she can focus closely on her work, for which she also needs her husband's permission. Similarly, Hertha in *The Half-Life of Marie Curie* expresses dissatisfaction at the concept of *femme covert*, according to which 'married women are technically property of their husbands and not legal persons under the – you know – law' (2022: 22), which, for instance, disqualified her from being a member of the Royal Society of Engineers: 'as soon as they found out I was the Ayrton in the skirt they rejected me all over again' (2022: 22). The play also shows the devastating effects that Marie's affair with Paul Lagevin had on her career, even though she was a widow then. Double moral standards are exposed: 'Goddamn the press for doing this to you. They wouldn't do this to a man' (2022: 10) and 'Men get to have sex all the time. They don't mind what Einstein does with his evenings. [. . . Y]ou must be perfect and saintly and untouched, while the men do exactly as they please' (2022: 14), claims Hertha. The play shows how Marie's career is endangered as she sees funding for her research being withdrawn and even the Nobel Committee asks her not to attend the ceremony. The celebration of the scientific achievements of these women scientists in Gunderson's history plays gains further significance when read against their contexts. Their difficult personal lives, corseted by patriarchal dictums, as well as their health conditions (the three of them struggle with cancer), are also brought to the stage. In their fight against sexism in science, Gunderson's female scientists also fight sexism in society at large. Their achievements in science are also achievements in women's struggle for equality.

In her historiographic approach, Gunderson does not present these women as if they were relics from the past. She builds for them a lasting legacy embodied in the form of the plays. These three plays are mainly realistic, but as has become customary also in science plays, they challenge the notion of realism. As Shepherd- Barr has noted,

> It is an interesting paradox of science plays that they are both 'old' and 'new' in their use of realism. Much of the dramatic core of science plays revolves around a conflict (or several conflicts), and since conflict traditionally has been the driving force of plays, science plays are traditional in that sense. (2006: 41)

These plays by Gunderson are 'old' in their approach to conflict, mostly developed linearly, and the stagings of the plays are usually maximalist in period accuracy as regards costume and scenery. The language Gunderson uses, though, is contemporary, speaking to present-day audiences (David 2017), and the endings, as those favoured by more radical feminist playmakers, are 'new' in dismantling realistic conventions. In these three plays the female protagonists talk from their afterlife, sometimes directly to the audience, dismantling the fourth wall. In their final words, they write their own stories and highlight their legacies, bringing together past and present (Kemper 2017, Wren 2019). Critics have found these plays didactic, entertaining, and moving, some identifying the feminism behind it, though their style may not be 'as inventive as the women [Gunderson] celebrates' (Snook 2019). Gunderson's historiographical hybrid realism seems not to be satisfactory for those who want more than a celebration of women's achievements and verbal denunciations of patriarchal oppression in the past.

Gunderson's most overtly experimental history plays provide sounder ground for discussion about what is expected from a feminist history play nowadays. Before turning to these more conventional plays on the history of women scientists, earlier in her career, Gunderson had written a very experimental piece to contribute to Herstory: *Emilie: La Marquise du Châtelet Defends Her Life Tonight* (2009). The protagonist is Emilie du Châtelet, the French seventeenth-century mathematician, physicist, and philosopher, for decades better known as the mistress and collaborator of Voltaire. Her *Institutions de Physique* (1740) became a landmark in Physics, as well as her translation of Isaac Newton's *Philosophiae Naturalis Principia Mathematica* (1687), to which she also contributed with a groundbreaking commentary on energy, and its quantitative relationships to the mass and velocity of an object.

Shepherd-Barr has identified a new kind of science play, the one that goes beyond the biography of the scientist to show the performance of science itself.

Necessarily, these plays get farther and farther away from realism (2006: 48). *Emilie* falls into this category. In this play, Gunderson makes use of one of the commonest devices in these science plays: metatheatre. The play opens in darkness, just a spotlight on Emilie, who in direct address to the audience announces she is dead but that she is not done yet. In control of her story, she retells stories of her past which are acted by another character, Soubrette. The re-enactment of scenes of her past are announced with 'the scene in which . . .' If Emilie touches characters from her past, lights flicker, and a blackout signals the forced end of that scene. Other experimental devices include double and triple casting and the use of tableaux. The non-linear experiment reveals critiques also found in the three plays already discussed: women's exploitation by men who take credit for women's work, the gender bias operating in science, and women's primary role as mothers and wives. Emilie is presented as a breaker of rules in her life, in her love relations and in her work. During the play, Emilie advocates for the validity of Leibniz's Living Force ($F = mv^2$), opposed to Newton's principle ($F = mv$), which came to be known as Dead Force. Her defence takes place along her tally between Love and Philosophy in her life. Emilie is 'not done' till Einstein, drawing on her work, develops his revolutionary formula $E = mc^2$ and she is given full recognition.

In watching the re-enactment of Emilie's story one finds a stunning combination of mathematics, philosophy, and theatricality. The play demonstrates the very concepts it deals with and takes the genre of history of science drama to the next level. Watching it we witness the wealth of ideas and abstractions that are brought to life through the material possibilities of the stage. The problem of explaining the science directly to the audience is skilfully handled by Gunderson's sense of drama and timing: her characters use short, direct sentences rather than long ones; she uses lots of repetitions, visual aids (Emilie writes and draws diagrams on the walls), demonstrations with actors' bodies, and figurative language. Indeed, the play's structure and its staging stand as a metaphor for Living Force itself. The mixture of past and present on the stage mirrors the relativity of Time and Space, which depends on Emilie, the observer. Living Force, a forerunner to kinetic energy, is used to organize the plot, provoking its acceleration leading up to the climax, when Emilie gives birth to her son and finishes her work on Newton. She dies shortly after, but she goes on alive, as her energy has simply transformed into her legacy, expressed in the open ending of the play with her last word followed by ellipsis: 'And . . .'

Critics are overtly divided as regards Gunderson's success in revisiting the story of Emilie du Châtelet in such experimental form. For Dubiner, Gunderson 'walks us through science and math which might be daunting to most people. She does this with assurance and deftness that lets us feel as smart as our heroine' (2024: 2). Similarly, Betsyann Faiella finds it an 'incredibly stylish work featuring the history of a real woman' (2023) and Susan Brall remarks that in the 'recent surge in dramas about remarkable women [... the play] stands tall' (2018). In contrast, Rhoda Feng, for the *New York Times*, finds the experimental devices 'prosaic' and not 'piquant' (2023), and other reviewers have also found the episodic structure 'formalized' till it becomes 'stiff', and just not 'entertaining' (Onofri 2023, Williams 2017). Some of the negative reviews make it evident that the way Gunderson has integrated science into the structure of the play, as scientific ideas are integral to the story and not a background, has not been fully grasped. Kirsten Shepherd-Barr has noted that 'One might say that the further science plays get from realism, the closer they get to real science; and the more compelling the science play, the more it tends to depart from straight realism' (2006: 43). In the face of the reception of *Emilie*, one wonders if Gunderson's feminist goal in revisiting a woman scientist lost to history would reach wider audiences if she had opted earlier for hybrid realism. The critiques that her other experimental play dealing with historical women, *The Revolutionists* (2018), has garnered seems to point in that direction as well.

Strictly speaking, *The Revolutionists* is not a history play, but a historiographical performance, staging a revision of the act of writing history. The historical setting, 1793 France during the Reign of Terror, allows Gunderson to imagine the meeting of four women. Three of them really existed, while one is invented. The 'badass' women, as Gunderson calls them, that people this play are playwright Olympe de Gouges, queen Marie Antoinette, the slayer of Jean-Paul Marat Charlotte Corday, and Marianne Angelle, a fictional Caribbean abolitionist leader and spy. The motive that brings them together is not the Revolution itself, but how histories of the Revolution will describe them. Marianne, Marie Antoinette, and Charlotte are tentative about the way history will write their legacies, so they search for Olympe, 'being confident she will do more justice than a man' (Smith 2016). They need to change what is 'known' about them, that is, the way patriarchal history has defined them and their actions, to a version where they are given a voice to express themselves. Marianne wants Olympe to write for the Revolution in the Caribbean 'to help people understand what we're fighting for, freedom, justice, humanity' (2018: 9). Aware of the magnitude of her actions and the impact she will have in the future, Charlotte is in desperate need of a female writer:

> *I don't have time for another time and/or never.* I have a guy to murder, which will land me on the scaffold, which is why I came to you . . . I NEED A LINE. My actions will be talked about for centuries and I don't want to sound like a

dingbat. I need something that will sink into their memories for all time, something with a lot of 'fuck you' in it. So. Playwright. Write. (2018: 14, emphasis in original)

Similarly, Queen Marie Antoinette, a female figure notably vilified in French history, comes in search of Olympe because she needs 'a rewrite' and 'some good press' (2018: 22). The character of Olympe, thus, emerges as the feminist playmaker historiographer, one through which Gunderson herself speaks: 'I know that our voices deserve the stage. We deserve to be our own heroes, everyone's heroes. We're all of us more alike than we are different, and if this revolution is what I think it is, this is the time to be known, and heard' (2018: 27). Writing about women who deserve a stage is not a choice, but a necessity. At a point when Olympe is about to destroy the play she is writing about them, Marianne reminds her that 'if you destroy them you destroy Charlotte and Marie and me. You destroy me. Because no one writes me down. . . . If you burn this story then everything we have fought for, everything that has happened, *every single person that has thrown their life into this will be as blank and mute as the paper you can't seem to fill*' (2018: 55, emphasis in original). Marianne further reminds her of the need to 'listen' to write 'what's real' because that is her 'power' (2018: 56, see Figure 3). The lines define Gunderson's belief in feminist artivism.

The way Gunderson complicates the notion of history as what is real in the play bears little resemblance to what has transcended as 'reality'. Hers is an imaginative exercise of what could have happened that invites to reconsider the writing of history and its enduring legacy. Her research is very obvious (Lyman 2016). She repeats and revises very well-known historical events, including the testing of the virginity and the execution of Charlotte Corday and the trial of Marie Antoinette. Gunderson recreates their executions, at the hands of an overtly symbolic character called Fraternité, with linguistic accuracy. But 'Gunderson reframes their famous last words in a way that sketches them as less sensational and controversial and more well-meaning and sincere' (Smith 2016). Charlotte's last words are 'I killed a man to save a thousand', a line in the play Olympe has written for her, while Marie Antoinette apologizes for stepping on the executioner's foot: 'I'm sorry, I did not mean to' (2018: 60). But in her re-enactment Gunderson imagines what these women would have felt and has them voice it. Charlotte would rather go with 'May God have no pity, you motherfuckers' (2018: 29), while Marie Antoinette wishes her 'last words are sympathetic. I just don't want to sound silly because I AM STILL THE GODDAM QUEEN OF FRANCE NO MATTER WHAT THOSE FUCKERS

Figure 3 Kenita R. Miller as Marianne Angelle and Lise Bruneau as Olympe de Gouges in the Cincinnati Playhouse in the Park's world premiere production of *The Revolutionists*. (Courtesy photo by Mikki Schaffner.[4])

SAY. And I. Will die. Royally' (2018: 30). While the accident with Fraternité does not allow Marie Antoinette to have this dignified death she had dreamt of, in her reimagining of her trial, Gunderson allows her character to speak her feelings, making her a protofeminist at the same time. Upon being sentenced to death, Marie Antoinette addresses men and asks them to 'remove the squint from your eyes so that you may fully see with whom you are dealing': a woman, a mother, and a queen citizen, not the heartless and unnatural woman in historical discourse. Furthermore, Marie Antoinette is fierce in her defence against historical charges of incest with her son: 'NOW YOU LISTEN HERE. YOU MAY PUSH ME BUT DO NOT PUSH MY CHILDREN, NEVER MY CHILDREN, YOU DO NOT SLANDER CHILDREN. The accusation is a disgusting lie that you dreamt up, not me, which says a lot more about the dreamer than it does about the accused you sick, pardon my American, DICKS' (2018: 58).

The reconstruction of historical scenes like this, based on Gunderson's imagining of these historical figures' feelings through twenty-first-century

---

[4] *The Revolutionists* was commissioned and first produced by the Cincinnati Playhouse in the Park in 2016. Full credits: Elaine Holdridge (director), Marion Williams (costume and set designer), Mark Barton (lighting designer), Andrea L. Shell (stage manager), Blake Robison (artistic director), Buzz Ward (managing director).

colloquial language, many times in vulgar language that has shocked reviewers (Dallas 2016), shows her approach to history is that of fictional recreation. But this playful recreation is also political, as Gunderson makes clear that then *any* version of history is fictional:

> OLYMPE: Story is the heartbeat of humanity and humanity gets really dark when the wrong stories are leading the people.
> CHARLOTTE: Well, I'm not here to make a *story*, I'm here to make *history*.
> OLYMPE: History *is* a story. Just with … an extra … 'hi.' … (*Using her hand as a puppet.*) Hi, Story! (2018: 16, emphasis in original)

Olympe, Gunderson's spokesperson, voices feminist approaches to the male-dominated version of history as fiction and, as such, one that can be rewritten. New versions, Gunderson says, are to be welcomed with a 'hi'. The fictional nature of her approach to history is also evident in the main device in the play: metatheatre. The four women collaborate in putting together the material for Olympe's play. Such a playful approach to history has not met the approval of all reviewers, who have found the play confusing about historical facts and faulty as regards its form. 'Gunderson confusingly blends real biographies with imagined ones and doesn't provide a ton of context for what is going on,' writes Tresca (2022), a critique present in other reviews (Clay 2017, Dallas 2016, Lyman 2016). Others, however, write that the play is not meant to be read as history, but as a piece of fiction 'about the way history writes women as crazy, violent and heretical, instead of as smart, forward-thinking and powerful' (Smith 2016). Significantly, those reviews which deny the worth of Gunderson's historiography for being untrue to facts commonly find metatheatre in the play tedious and its genre confusing (Clay 2017, Dallas 2016).

Gunderson's rejection of an objective account of history is backed up by a rejection of formal strictures in *The Revolutionists*. The play seems to follow linear development until, towards the end of the play, it turns into a circular structure. The play is revealed to be taking place within Olympe's mind as she is walking her way to the scaffold where she is going to be executed. With the help of Marianne, Olympe narrates her own death. As in her other history plays, Gunderson writes an open ending, and once Olympe is executed, she addresses the audience to tell us 'And a story … begins' (2018: 71). Her death as the beginning of a story is an invitation to write stories about her, as male-dominated history has done. The fictionality and multiplicity of possibilities to write stories are evident in the play's subtitle: 'A Comedy, a Quartet, a Revolutionary Dream Fugue, and A True Story', a subtitle some might find confusing as regards the play's style. The subtitle, however, is pretty accurate in describing the play. The comedic genre tells of the fictional recreation of the 'true story' behind her characters. The use of songs in the play is announced in both the quartet and the dream fugue. After each execution, the four women come together in singing a feminist historiographical hymn which includes the key line, 'Who are we, without a story'. The quartet also suggests that the four female voices of the play will be heard – unlike those versions of history which have silenced them. The polyvocality of this approach is also suggested in the revolutionary dream fugue. The musical metaphor signals the repetition of themes by the successively entering voices, which develop contrapuntally. And so, Marianne's, Olympe's, Marie Antoinette's, and Charlotte's voices are meant to denounce sexism in male-dominated history and their victimization at the hands of sexism, classism, and racism.

One of the most problematic aspects of Gunderson's feminist historiography relates to how she deals with the representation of women of colour. This has been a polemical issue for feminists, especially in the second wave, and is also alive in debates on history. In *The Revolutionists*, several critics point out that, 'notably, the play's sole black character is an amalgamation of several people rather than a fully-fledged historical woman with a lived biography' (Tresca 2022). Being repeatedly asked about why Marianne is the only fictional character, when the other white characters are fully fledged historical women with biographies, Gunderson replied that it is because all the women are inside Olympe's mind. Consequently, as Olympe did know Marie Antoinette and it is very probable that she had heard and read of Charlotte, these two are historical figures that Olympe can incorporate into her play. In contrast, Gunderson argues, Olympe has to invent Marianne because she would not have known any San Dominguean/Haitian freedom fighters. Gunderson continues,

> Marianne was created in Olympe's mind from what she did know: that the French were fighting a civil war for freedom while hypocritically colonizing and enslaving people on the island of San Domingue, those people who were rebelling for their freedom and led by men and women of bravery and intelligence, those people were winning. To Olympe this is the ideal of liberation, coupled with a confrontation of a hypocrisy at the core of French Revolutionary leadership: they are calling their fight a fight for freedom, yet they violently enslave Black people oceans away and subjugate women all across France. This is why she invents Marianne (which is also the name of the iconic French symbol of freedom in *Liberty Leading the People* (*La Liberté guidant le peuple* by Eugène Delacroix). (Gunderson nd)

Marianne's use as a symbol of female power and struggle for freedom and equality is very evident in the play. She is present to denounce the hypocrisy of the leaders of French Revolution and their *Liberté, Egalité* and *Fraternité*, hypocrisy which resonates in the play with the American Declaration of Independence and its blatant denial of the rights of women as well. Gunderson's need to justify at length the creation of this character, however, reveals anxieties as regards who can write about certain characters and in what ways.

Furthermore, Gunderson's alleged need to invent Marianne becomes more problematic in the way this character joins that sisterhood against patriarchy proposed in *The Revolutionists*. Gunderson makes use of Marianne to reveal race prejudices in the past that might still be working in the present. Marianne's line 'no one writes me down' signifies the general marginalization and silencing black women have been subjugated to. Through the opposition between the characters of Marie Antoinette and Marianne, Gunderson enacts prevailing white supremacy:

> MARIE: You know it's the funniest thing, when I walked in here I could have sworn that you were my servant –
> MARIANNE: I AM A FREE WOMAN OF MEANS LIKE YOU AND YOU AND YOU. I AM NO ONE'S SERVANT, I'M JUST STANDING NEARBY.
> (2018: 24)

The difficult relation between these two is constant until mid the play, when in a forced romantic turn, they become friends by means of what they have in common as women, regardless their ethnicity or class: that they loved their husbands (now dead), that they love, miss, and would do anything to protect their children, and that 'work-life balance' is hard for them (2018: 34–38). Sisterhood as a means to debunk patriarchal approaches to history and patriarchy as a political system have worked in *Silent Sky* and *The Half-Life of Marie Curie*, where the historical figures, regardless of race in the choice of cast for performances, have remained white. In *The Revolutionists*, however, the way Gunderson manages ethnic differences among women, when dealing with such a poignant theme as slavery, does not seem altogether satisfactory. Discomfort has been noted by critics. Although a fictional recreation, this play's political aim calls for a more profound consideration of the struggles of women of colour and the means to bring together women, regardless of colour, in the fight against patriarchal prejudices.

As seen, Gunderson's revision of history follows the path of second-wave feminists in bringing centre stage and celebrating women lost to male-dominated versions of history. At the same time, these women's stories are employed to alert to gender biases not only in history writing, but in the world at large. Gunderson seems supportive of the notion of sisterhood in ways that remind of the second wave and that, accounting for the reception of her plays, remains problematic when race is involved. Her theatrical historiographical practice remains 'in between'. Hybrid realistic pieces are favoured by critics and the general public alike. Her more experimental pieces, which rely heavily on metatheatre to expose the fictionality behind history writing, signal to a problematic 'new direction' in her practice. Her latest history play, *Artemisia* (2023), on Renaissance painter Artemisia Gentileschi, marks Gunderson's return to hybrid realism. This playwright's imagination can take her somewhere else for her next history play, but this play's reception reveals, once again, a more general approval of this form (Falkenstein 2023, Fischer 2023).

3 Feminist Approach to the Medical Humanities: On Women and Illness

In recent years, we have borne witness to the growth of the Medical Humanities, an interdisciplinary field of enquiry that applies the perspectives and methodologies of the arts, the humanities, and the social sciences to medical education and practice. The overall aim of this discipline is to humanize medical practices which, due to the commodification of health systems and the successes of modern medicine, above all as regards biotechnology, have resulted in the reduction of patients to their disease. The pivotal works of Arthur Kleiman made a necessary distinction between disease and illness (1980, 1986). Disease is a biomedical category and diagnostic entity, for which medical and technical solutions are sought. In this paradigm the patient becomes the object of professional inquiry. In contrast, illness is a biopsychosocial category that brings together the body, the self, and society at large. 'Biomedicine itself is rooted in male dominance, or patriarchy' (Sharma 2019: 570) and as such 'does not relate to a cultural context that refers only to men, but refers to a dominant cultural form based on a particular kind of logic that embraces heroism, rationalism, certainty, the intellect, distance, objectification, and explanation before appreciation' (Bleakley 2013: 47). Such gender bias in a male dominated medical enterprise has 'frequently patronized women and their experiences, and placed little value on their lived experiences and expertise' (Sharma 2019: 572). The women's health movement, which emerged during the second wave of feminism, challenged such an authoritative position of the healthcare system, cherishing women's experiences and demanding improved healthcare and the end of sexism in healthcare systems. 'Activists fought to empower women's knowledge, gain control over reproduction rights, and reclaim power from the paternalistic medical community' (Shai et al. 2021: 1). The publication of *Our Bodies, Ourselves*, by Boston's Women's Health Collective in 1971 was a landmark. Frank in its treatment of women's sexuality, the book was conceived 'as a model for women to learn about themselves, communicate their findings with doctors, and challenge the medical establishment to change and improve the care that women receive' (Our Bodies Ourselves Today). *Our Bodies, Ourselves* has been revised and updated for over forty years, translated into multiple languages, and sold millions of copies, which only shows how this issue, initiated in the 1960s, is still urgent nowadays.

Feminism has long informed the endeavour of the Medical Humanities to create dialogue between medical research, practices, and the humanities. Feminist approaches, as Foster and Funke have stated, 'have helped to develop alternative understandings of health, illness, and the body, and to identify intersections between the humanities and biomedicine' even if the scholars who explicitly acknowledge their debt to feminism are still scarce in the field of Medical Humanities (2018: 1). Well into the twenty-first century, many scholars go on claiming the need of a feminist lens to make visible the specific ways in which women relate to health and illness and to 'champion alternative modes of expression, including the creative arts, to understand embodied experience' (2018: 2).

For decades, the creative arts had been considered a 'supportive friend' (Brody 2011) or a 'handmaiden' to medicine (Bleakley 2015: 2). Moving on to another stage in the Medical Humanities, the creative arts have started to receive the critical and practical attention deserved. If in the early days of the field, humanities' value was as a tool to train more empathetic doctors, now they are seen as viable ways for patients to gain agency, for health professionals to reach diagnosis or to help shape a society more understanding of certain pathologies, among other uses. The value of theatre for medical purposes has a long history. As Stanton B. Garner, Jr. has argued, 'As a medium comprised of living, breathing bodies, theatre has long concerned itself with illness, medical theory and practice, and the institutions associated with them.' On the other hand: 'For their part, those inside and on the fringes of the medical profession have often looked to theatre for models of medical demonstration, observation and training' (2023: 2, 3). Furthermore, the intrinsic and potential value of theatre for the Medical Humanities is implied in Garner's description of how 'theatre empowers the embodied subject, allowing it to express itself in an intersubjective field with other individuals on stage and off... In this overt way, theatre undermines scientific medicine's tendency to reduce illness to a psycho-chemical problem and the patient to a scientific case study' (2020: 96). Going one step further, and in a statement especially significant for feminist practices, Mermikides and Bouchard have also acknowledged that, in performance, 'Bodies can be staged in ways that draw attention to the potentially brutalizing effects of treating subjects as specimens and it can establish a dynamic of care and ethics of spectatorship that runs against persistence of objectifying medical vision and intrusive revelation' (2016: 4).

Theatre practitioners' interest in staging ill bodies on the stage has lately been met by the audience's demand. The late twentieth century saw the emergence of theatre as a growing area of science-arts practice, and, specifically, theatre that engages 'medicine or medical science represent[s] a particularly vibrant subgenre of science-engaged performance' (Mermikides and Bouchard 2016: 6–7). Analogous to the contribution of feminism to the Medical Humanities, as discussed earlier, US women playwrights have paralleled this trend, using the stage to bring attention to the intersections of gender, illness, and medical care, as seen in much acclaimed plays such as Margaret Edson's *W;t* (1999), Sarah Ruhl's *The Clean House* (2004), or Peggy Shaw's *Ruff* (2012). Lauren Gunderson openly approaches health and illness through a gendered lens in a number of plays where characters perform different roles of interest for the Medical Humanities, from patients and their relatives to health professionals.

Patients' voices are especially heard in what Ann Hunsaker Hawkins has called pathography, a subgenre of autobiography pivotal within the Medical Humanities. The telling of 'the story of illness from the perspective of the individual patient' (1999: 128) is an empowering tool, one that allows the patient to regain control over their sick body and to resist the usual objectification and victimization to the medical system (Couser 1997: 12). In the way Gunderson tells her protagonists' experiences from their own perspectives, her plays can be considered pathographies. In her earliest medical play, the unpublished one-woman show *Last Tape* (2004), the character of Woman comes into terms with her mortality and cancer by talking to herself through a tape. The audience first sees her recording the first part of a conversation. Her voice, '*young and naïve*' (2004: 1) is one unaware of her illness. Once the process of recording herself is over, Woman, now '*weathered but not bitter*' (2004: 1), talks to her recorded self, showing her control over voicing the news of cancer and her acceptance of mortality. Recording her autopathography becomes a theatrical event where she is the protagonist. This play, an adaptation of Beckett's *Krapp's Last Tape* (1958), makes use of playing a cassette as a metaphor for life. Woman records and talks to herself as proof of existence and control, to the point that it is Woman who stops the tape and decides to play music instead in the end. In contrast with Beckett's impending silence at the end of his play, commonly interpreted as death faced by the aging protagonist,

Woman's acceptance of her own death is loud, as she decides to play music instead.

Krapp is not the only aging protagonist that inspires Gunderson in her medical works. King Lear, whose importance for the Medical Humanities has already been explored as an example of dementia (Chansky 2023: 3), plays a pivotal role in her autobiographical piece *The Heath*, developed at Berkeley Rep's Ground Floor in 2013. Gunderson has described the play as a solo play with two characters (2020f). The character of Lauren, a woman in her thirties, embodies the playwright herself, while Actor, a man in his eighties, plays her grandfather, KD, who suffered from Alzheimer's disease and passed away, and King Lear. As typical in many pathographies, the play is didactic as regards Alzheimer's. Projections and subtitles are used to explain how memory works, while the Actor as KD and King Lear performs some of Alzheimer's disease symptoms, both mental and physical, and its stages.

In her inspiring work *Illness as Metaphor* (1978), Susan Sontag challenged metaphors often used to describe illnesses and the people affected by them. The popularization of commonplace metaphors – such as 'invasive cancer cells' or 'to fight against a disease' – loses their power to cause an impact by their overuse. In the case of Alzheimer's disease, this is commonly presented as a stealer of memories (Chansky 2023: 29). Gunderson, inspired by Shakespeare, contributes to the Medical Humanities with a new metaphor. The storm, that incredible force of nature in *King Lear*, symbolizes the disease itself and more:

> The storm represents the tumult and uncertainty of my grandfather's Alzheimer's disease, the damage that it can do to a family, the unpredictable sadness and 'natural disaster' of dementia. It also represents what I feel as my betrayal of my grandfather by not showing up for him enough when he was sick. His disease and death was a storm, and survivors like me are often left with the emotional wreckage afterwards. (in 'Q&A: Playwright Lauren Gunderson' 2019)

Moreover, the storm is used as a structuring device, repeated through the play, amplifying its meanings each time. The storm is heard when Lauren and Actor talk about the Second World War (as KD fought there and was made prisoner), and it is also heard in the background when staging moments of loneliness, madness, and death itself. The heath in the title is also an interesting metaphor borrowed from Shakespeare, that wasteland that offers no protection from the storm is the location from which Lauren sees the storm coming, happening, and where she is left. As a whole, and especially through these metaphors, with *The Heath*, Gunderson challenges dominant cultural understandings of dementia, one of the key strategies of performative pathographies according to Brodzinski (2016), forcing the audience to see what patients may be feeling and thinking and its impact on patients and families.

Gunderson's theatrical use of her grandfather's illness blurs the boundary between biography and autobiography. It is plain to realize that Gunderson's strategy to counter her grandfather's memory loss is to write about his life, so that this is never forgotten: 'A body ends. A story doesn't. If we keep telling it' (2020: 96). At the same time, *The Heath* is an autopathography; it is Gunderson's way of dealing with her grandfather's illness, with the fear that her future may resemble his, and a catharsis for not showing up:

> And will I know myself when I go – and will I have control – and will I have a legacy – and will I be remembered – and will I be happy – and will someone read to me when I'm dying? And will someone sing to me? And will someone help me through it? Will someone be better to me than I was to him?' (2020: 86)

Remorseful that she could not stand to see KD's deterioration, that she walked away and did not even attend his funeral, the play stages those conversations she never had with KD. Furthermore, performance allows Lauren to be by her grandfather the moment he dies:

> LAUREN: I'm here, I'm here.
> *(She stops, looks at him and starts to hear his final moments . . . .)*
> *((RECORDING – Sherry's story of KD's death))*
> *(During the recording Lauren imitates Sherry's action . . .*
> *Pull the cover up*
> *Rub his legs*
> *Other side of the bed*
> *Sit beside him*
> *Hold his hand*
> *Close her eyes*
> *Pray*
> *Open up her eyes*
> *He inhales*
> *Never exhales . . .)*
>
> (2020: 94)

During the performance, the reproduction of the actual recording where Sherry, taking care of KD then, describes his last moments allows Lauren to embody and thank her and to be with her grandfather till his last breath. By itself, the recording celebrates the key role of health professionals and carers who assist kindly and lovingly towards those in terminal conditions, providing comfort to the dying and their relatives. While the play is confessional, there is also a political dimension to it that Gunderson does not forget to mention in discussing the play:

> He wasn't the same man anymore. In many ways I felt terrible for him because I know he'd not want to be remembered in such a state. It's heartbreaking. This is the reality and urgency of Alzheimer's and dementia research. If we could find a solution to these deteriorating diseases of the mind, it would be such a gift to the world. It would give dignity back to so many. It would save so many lives and families. (in 'Q&A: Playwright Lauren Gunderson' 2019)

Gunderson openly demands urgent research on dementia and to treat these people with dignity, which for her implies bringing humanity to a medical condition: 'Show up. Be present. Play music. Tell stories. Get them talking and record it. Say I love you' (in 'Q&A: Playwright Lauren Gunderson' 2019). The play's intention to reach out also shows in the organization of talkbacks and panels on aging and dementia to accompany the production of the play, as has been the case in the professional productions of *The Heath* so far, at the Merrimack Theatre in 2018 and at the Warehouse Theatre in 2019. Reviews, of these productions as well as the audio version featuring the author and John Larroquete, have applauded the lyrical weaving of science, *King Lear* and confession, resulting in a 'magic', 'powerful' piece (Shurley 2020) with 'cloudbursts of wisdom and insights about matters of contemporary life that matter deeply (or should) to all of us' (Paine 2021).

Compared to her first medical piece, *Last Tape*, a realistic piece that plays with the technology of the tape recorder in ways similar to Beckett back in 1958, *The Heath* is more experimental. The projection of titles for each scene and of numerous pictures, its metatheatrical essence, together with the playing of Sherry's recording and many musical pieces on the banjo, makes *The Heath* an innovative piece, unlimited to traditional genre definitions. Nevertheless, in bringing together science and theatre, both plays can be considered conservative. Borrowing Mermikides and Bouchard's words, *Last Tape* and *The Heath* serve 'a 'public engagement' agenda, using drama's ability to provoke emotional engagement to raise interest' in the illness presented (2016: 9). Much more alternative forms are found in *The Catastrophist* and *I and You*, plays with which Gunderson joins 'a tendency to experiment with formal innovations that culminates in the newer science plays of the late twentieth and early twenty-first centuries' (Shepherd-Barr 2006: 39).

I and You is the play that catapulted Gunderson into popularity in 2013. It won the American Theatre Critics Association New Play award, it was a Susan Smith Blackburn Prize Finalist in 2014, Methuen prestigious collection of

Modern Classics published it in 2021, and, thanks in no small part to this play, Gunderson became the most produced playwright in the United States in the seasons 2016–2017 and 2019–2020. Besides its popularity in the United States, *I and You* was produced at the London Hampstead Theatre in 2018, where it also garnered much public attention, featuring *Game of Thrones* star Maisie Williams in its lead role. The protagonist is a rare find in mainstream theatre, one that gives voice to young female patients. Following what apparently is a naturalistic well-made play, the first act introduces us to the conflict. Caroline is homebound because her liver's malfunction has worsened to the point she cannot attend school anymore. Her only hope is the donor waiting list, that list on which nearly one in ten patients dies (Wiesler 2014: 519). Her classmate Anthony, whom she had not met before, comes home because their project on Whitman's use of pronouns in *Song of Myself* is due next day. She is reluctant to accept him in her room, and during the first and second acts, following the Aristotelian pattern, the conflict becomes more complicated. They do not seem to agree on their project and Caroline's anxieties are revealed, including her fear of death and her isolation:

> This is my room, this is my phone, I've been sick pretty much ever since I was born. That's me. Yawp... They tried a ton of stuff and now we're at the point where I just need a new thing. So I wait. But I'm a pretty good candidate because I'm young and I came by this crap honestly (it's genetic, yay!). Anyway 'livers are a robust organ' so it's not as sketchy as it can be, but the whole process is kinda crazy, so my life is kinda crazy, so I'm kinda crazy. Like I've always been *kinda* sick but not you-can't-go-to-school sick, which sucks like so much. I mean I'm a *senior*. I have crucial things to do and then, out of the blue, my house is like this crappy clinic and my mom is on constant red alert and everything is so weird now. (2021a: 27–28, emphasis in original)

In her medicalized room, the audience understands the physical and psychological burdens of Caroline's illness, how tired she is of treatments, of feeling patronized by doctors and her mother, and how she feels singled out socially because of her condition. The third act, finally, includes the climatic turning point leading to the resolution of the conflict: Caroline and Anthony are fully connected, and the project is finalized. But the naturalistic approach of the play is suddenly disrupted by one of Gunderson's favourite devices: a Brechtian-like twist in the plot.

Towards the end of the play, the fire alarm, almost inaudible throughout the play but steadily present, starts beeping louder and louder. The walls start to vanish as Anthony says 'There is nothing here. But you and I.' The beeps get closer together 'more and more like their true nature, which is a heart monitor [... T]he final wall, the floor, the world of her room vanishes, falls, flies away.

Infinite blackness all around. Her breath is echoed, volumized all around her. He leaves her side' (2021a: 74). This twist reveals that the whole play has taken place in a dream space, while Caroline has been under the effects of anaesthesia. Anthony explains

> You got a call today, 'There's a donor.' . . . Your bag was packed,
> you were ready for this
> your mom drove you to the hospital,
> and I was already there,
> they sped you into surgery,
> and I was already there,
> the surgery went well,
> you're coming out of it right now,
> you're doing fine,
> and you'll wake up soon,
> and I'm already there. . . .
> I wanted to meet you.
> And see how we can make this work.
> And it will. (2021a: 73)

Gunderson's choice to subvert naturalism and provide the climax with this twist is shocking and effective. Such a rupture in the audience's suspension of disbelief demands a revision of the plot so far, an understanding of how a medical idea has been used as an extended metaphor. The setting of the room has always been Caroline's body and the action a metaphor for liver transplant surgery. Roger Kneebone has affirmed that in performing surgery, with emphasis on the first term of the collocation, the patient '*as a person* disappears from view, as attention is narrowed to physical aspects of the body' (2016: 70, emphasis in original). In her performance of surgery, Gunderson gives the patient her leading role, showing her active during the surgery.

The medical difficulties in adjusting an alien liver to a new body are embodied in Caroline's and Anthony's polarized features: a girl and a boy of different ethnicities, the nerd and the popular basketball star with very opposed tastes in music and hobbies. At the medical level, as the two characters bridge their differences and navigate the complexities of human connection, this reads as the process of transplantation and its many complications. Thus, Caroline's initial defence of her room, naturalistically and medically understood as typical of the isolated teenage patient, now typifies the body's initial rejection of a transplanted organ. Once Caroline starts trusting and befriending Anthony, and they start working on the project, it seems the new liver is accommodating to the new body. A moment when Anthony wants to leave represents the organ resisting the biology of the new body. And the characters final embrace, 'a hard desperate hug – ... the culmination of everything' (2021a: 75) before Anthony vanishes, is a metaphor for the perfect union of his liver and her body, anatomical harmony and the eternal connection of two bodies, the ever-lasting bond between donor and transplanted patient. The play ends with a flood of light as Caroline is waking up from her surgery; her hopeful future lying ahead.

The success of *I and You* with audiences shows in its numerous productions and in many positive reviews. These usually reverberate with words such as 'emotions', 'surprise', and 'heart-warming' (Dickinson 2021, Wood 2018). These very qualities are, however, present in most negative reviews too. Writing for the *New York Times*, Ben Brantley called *I and You* a 'sentimental character study' (2016), and 'sentimentality' is also mentioned in Nelson Pressley's review for the *Washington Post* (2014). As regards the play's surprise factor, these reviewers find in the plot twist a defective device: 'the twist is not just shocking, it makes the play', wrote Jonathan Mandell for *DC Theatre Scene* (2016). Jesse Green for *Vulture* indicated that 'a wrench of a surprise thrown at us five minutes before the end renders everything that came before it moot' (2016), a remark shared by Michael Billington writing about the Hampstead Theatre production for *The Guardian*. For him, the play 'depends too heavily on a surprise ending' (2018). Taking all these reviews together, the existing gender bias in theatre reviewers seems evident. As Derr has put it, 'Though this emphasis on arousing emotion is as old as Aristotle, a review of the critical reception of Gunderson's major plays reveals that in the hands of a woman writer, deployed as a tool in telling women's stories, empathy becomes sentimentalism, and surprise becomes a deceptive trick' (2022: 74).

The style and structure of *I and You* are not defective but effective and illustrative of Gunderson's in-between feminist practice. The naturalistic style and Aristotelian structure move the audience towards Caroline. The Brechtian, alienating, ending, with the climatic twist in the plot that reveals what has really happened is not only cathartic, but also provides that place for hope that Dolan identifies in twenty-first-century feminist theatre in a very practical way. The ending constitutes a call for the audience to realize the importance of organ donation. Programs and productions so far have usually integrated information about the urgency of liver donation. Thus, *I and You* contributes to the Medical Humanities in very useful ways. In its translation of surgery to play structure, *I and You* also succeeds as a science play. And last but not least, it brings to the forefront a feminist agenda: the refocus on a young female patient and a feminist theatre of hope characterized by an appeal to 'universal goodness' (Edson and Gunderson 2014: 73).

Gunderson's feminist lens applied to pathography is most evident in her latest and most experimental medical piece: *The Catastrophist*. The play was commissioned by Marin Theatre Company during the 2020 lockdown and is based on the life and work of Dr Nathan Wolfe, a renowned virologist, author of *The Viral Storm*, and who is also Gunderson's husband. Written during the COVID-19 pandemic, it deals, however, with a former pandemic, as Dr Wolfe and his team had predicted the Ebola outbreak in 2014. The play includes a direct critique of governments' mishandling of experts' warnings of pandemics. Nathan, the protagonist, tells of his meeting with the head of the CDC (Centers for Disease Control and Prevention) in Washington DC in April 2014 to request taking measures to prevent the spread of Ebola in West Africa. Not only was the warning ignored, but months later Nathan and his team were 'accused of mishandling the Ebola outbreak' because they decided to help the people in Sierra Leone with the little resources they had. 'And rather than let us do our job to get the world ready for the next pandemic, we're forced to devote months of our time fighting this inane accusation' (2021b: 33, 41–42). From the medical point of view, the play provides glimpses of the hard work of virologists and the sometimes-difficult relations with those who take decisions, clearly suggesting that bureaucracy becomes one more obstacle in the handling of pandemics. The science part of the play is didactically explained by Nathan. Using diagrams, concepts such as eukaryotes, prokaryotes or the differences between virus and bacteria are explained. But besides this informative importance of the play within the Medical Humanities, making difficult notions understandable and even enjoyable during a performance, the play succeeds in keeping together the virologist and the man, who is a son, a husband, and a father.

The blending of the medical and the personal constitutes Gunderson's feminist intervention in her husband's pathography. While this is a solo play – Nathan is alone on a bare stage – the character of Lauren is absent and yet present. Many times Nathan is listening to Lauren and replying to her. He repeats her command to 'Keep going' in telling his story, and she is the one that provides the titles for the scenes, which made visible on the stage cue Nathan to talk. The play is built on the traditional metaphor 'Life is theatre', and the last scene reveals that this is indeed a play that Lauren is writing while Nathan is undergoing surgery. The setting, an '*undefined space he can't get out. It looks like a bare stage because it is*' (2021b: 3), is the space of Nathan's mind, one Gunderson uses to force her husband to see his work and his life as a continuum. Labour and the personal are fused as episodes from Nathan's work are mixed with personal and domestic realities. By providing the scene titles, Lauren the playwright forces Nathan to talk about 'Pandemics', 'Insurance', or 'Risk' but also about the death of his father ('Miami'), the births of his sons ('Charles' and 'Asa'), and his own heart condition ('Hospital'). Taken together, spectators get to know the health professional and his personal life, reminding us of the fact that health professionals, like everyone else, also have their own personal stories. For the character of Nathan, being forced to go through the ups and downs of his personal life helps him come to terms with his own humanity. Even though he is a futurist, he does 'not see his own future', and though a catastrophist, he cannot 'plan his own catastrophe' (2021b: 28).

Catastrophe as death interrupts the scenes through the appearance of the title 'Final Scene' several times ahead of the ending. Flashing lights announce this scene, making Nathan panic. And every time he struggles to keep control over the play, to keep talking, and to delay his end. This device, controlled by the playwright, is a signal of life's uncertainty, but also of the urgency to avoid catastrophes when these can be avoided somehow. Towards the end of the play, Lauren is mad at Nathan for ignoring the genetics of heart disease, as heart disease caused the death of his grandfather, his uncle, and his cousins before they were forty (2021b: 49). The real 'Final scene' takes place as Nathan is under the effects of anaesthesia, 'And because I am out of commission at present, she is in charge. Of my story' (2021b: 48). In Lauren's writing of the story, the real-life success of Nathan's heart surgery to amend the blockage of one of its arteries translates into music. The sound of a heart pumping is joined little by little by other heartbeats: Lauren's, their sons', Nathan's father's ... And the heartbeats keep adding up '*crashing into one another. Beautiful chaos. Life as percussion*' (2021b: 51). In this melodious ending science saves Nathan's life as much as the presence of those beloved ones, past and present.

The use of metatheatre, which has become one of the main devices in recent medical plays (Shepherd-Barr 2006: 180), allows Gunderson, not only to dismantle suspension of disbelief, but also, and at the same time, to create empathy and uplift emotion in the play. As Shepherd-Barr has said, 'the combination of direct address and enactment of theme is even more powerful ... because the situations are so ripe for empathy, so moving and visceral' (2006: 180). As seen in other plays, in her feminist writing Gunderson combines again alienating and experimental techniques with devices that prioritize emotions. Other devices Gunderson employs to bring the audience closer to the protagonist relate to the experiential play this is meant to be. Each audience member is encouraged to gather beeswax, coffee grounds, and a burnt match; props cued during the play, so that we sense what Nathan is sensing on stage. But perhaps the most basic strategy Gunderson has to foster emotions is by presenting the virologist as a family man. For instance, a decisive stage direction during his surgery brings together all these facets in a very sensorial way: '*Music rises, heart beat, trees in the forest, scuba diving, prayer, baby laughing, water boiling spoon tapping mug, gasp, typing*' (2021b: 50). His own heart struggling to beat is joined by the sound of trees in the forest of Cameroon where he conducted research, by his love for diving, his Jewish upbringing, by the laughs of his children, by the sound of his father having instant coffee and by the sound of his wife typewriting her plays. For the streamed performance produced by Marin Theatre Company and Round House, video footage collected such images of Nathan's life; described by a reviewer as 'an impactful theatrical tool' that makes this 'a real, affecting, human story and an important one at that' (Ell 2021). Other positive reviews have also highlighted the sensorial aspects and how successful the play is in presenting 'a poignant marriage of human experience and scientific reality that has significant social relevance' (Grogan 2021), highlighting also the personal, domestic, side of the scientist. In contrast, Peter Marks for the *Washington Post* finds the domestic aspects of *The Catastrophist* to be a digression from the successful parts of the play (2021), and Lily Janiak at the *San Francisco Chronicle* also devalues this play for being partly biographical (in Derr 2022: 74). Jesse Green, reviewing the play for the *New York Times*, sees that the glimpses of 'ordinary life' 'undermine the whole play', which he summarizes as 'essentially a promotional résumé, poetically phrased and embroidered with metatheatrical doodads' where the surprise ending, for one familiar with her works, is not surprising, but 'a fraud' (2021).

Reviews like these ones reveal the strict patterns some expect for medical plays, where the scientific and the personal, contrary to the notion of pathography central to Medical Humanities, should remain separate. Gunderson's feminist approach to the Medical Humanities remains as in-between problematic for critics as other of her works in how she prioritizes emotions over reason and in the degree of experimentation of her works. What seems undeniable is her zeal to bring female patients to the stage, to make her audience empathize with her protagonists, and, in sum, to make people *feel* her theatre in ways that make them react. Gunderson's words about her science plays seem pertinent: 'We need more stories that prove that real morality, real ethical behavior, real compassion and goodness and soulfulness works *with* science to better the *real* world, not the one trapped behind immovable and inflexible ideas that hold us back' (2015, emphasis in original). Speaking through Nathan, that rewritten version of her real-life husband in *The Catastrophist*, Gunderson says: 'Anyone can help to heal the world using the talents they've been blessed with. What will you do?' (2021b: 9).

4 Feminist Popular Entertainment

Arguably, one of the main reasons why some critics are negative about the quality of Gunderson's work is because she embraces popular genres (e.g. Christmas entertainment, romantic comedies) and, most recently, musicals.

These are often considered third-rate dramatic works: pure entertainment where experimentation and significant themes do not seem to have a place. A significant number of plays that keep Gunderson on that famous-most-produced-playwrights list are in fact mainstream shows; in particular, a cycle Gunderson has co-authored with Margot Melcon based on Jane Austen's *Pride and Prejudice*. Beginning in 2016 with *Miss Bennet (Christmas at Pemberley)*, the cycle has since included *The Wickhams* in 2019 and *Georgiana and Kitty* in 2022. In these, Gunderson and Melcon recreate the world of Austen's secondary and minor characters. The reasons that have led Gunderson to draw on Austen's works are enlightening about the playwright's strategy to make a living in the theatre and maintain her feminist ethos at the same time. Gunderson has been explicit in considering period adaptations 'a platform', a chance 'to be known and out there' (2020e). Her Austen cycle is a practical way to be produced, make a living, and continue writing. Moreover, a feminist drive is identified in making Jane Austen better known to contemporary audiences, which, as seen in Section 1, has been fundamental to the creation of a feminist literary canon. Gunderson has also stated that Austen inspired her feminist writing:

> As a young writer, I admired Austen's life as a writer as much as I admired her stories, with their unstoppable humor and literary observation. She wrote with grace and sharpness. She was funny and kind, romantic and wise, astute and fanciful, and put women at the center of timeless literature. She taught me that I could be and do the same. (2016)

This statement hints at why of all her works, the Austen cycle is clearly the most obvious example of her in-between feminism. Gunderson's approach slightly updates and brings forward Austen's protofeminism.

Unlike adaptations discussed in Section 1, Gunderson and Melcon's approach to Austen's *Pride and Prejudice* is historical and faithful to the original. Their feminist intervention is circumscribed by Austen's world itself in realistic terms. Austen's protofeminism is made evident and taken further in their sequels, but always within given forms of heteronormativity and acceptable revolutions. Although Gunderson has claimed she is 'allergic to the well-made play' (2020e), she makes overt use of the form and its identifiable ingredients. Lost and found letters, misunderstandings, orphanages, and a villain (Wickham, for obvious reasons) are all present in these three plays, all coming to happy resolutions, with two of them ending in weddings. The plays maintain the flavour, the language (including dialect), and even the humour of the Austen aura (Morin 2021), and offer a realistic feast for the eyes. All reviews mention the majestic Christmas tree that presides the stage, and productions are generous in festive details the scripts call for: colourful decorations, Christmas punch, orange cookies, and even snow and an impressive piano in *Miss Bennet* and *Georgiana and Kitty* (Holman 2018, Jones 2016). Adjectives such as 'sweet', 'pleasant', 'soapy', or 'clean' populate reviews, which suggests that the feminist drive of the plays might be sugar-coated (Holman 2018, Janiak 2016, Jones 2016).

Aston and Harris (2013) have reassessed the use of popular shows to 'entertain' and yet present a feminist outlook, claiming the need to get free of the critical grip on the popular and sentimental as a site of inferior cultural work. Specifically, Aston has argued the critical boundary between what is considered 'profitable', that is, of social value, and 'pleasurable', understood as a devalued form of theatre aligned with consumption and sheer pleasure (2013a: 24). I contend Gunderson and Melcon's cycle calls for reassessment as pieces of work that are profitable, pleasurable, and feminist in spirit. While it is true that the plays conform to heteronormativity, projecting an ordered world where women know how to make a home, dream of rearing children, and adore their husbands, the three plays manifest, as Austen's work did, women's need for economic independence, an issue that remains important today (Cordell 2021). Gunderson and Melcon invite us to remember that the marriage plots in *Pride and Prejudice* are driven by gender, by the fact that the Bennet sisters, being women, will not inherit their father's property and thus need to find husbands to provide for them. Mary, the protagonist in *Miss Bennet*, finds herself in that same critical position. And as Lizzy and Jane before her, she will find a good match; in her case, in Arthur de Bourgh. Arthur, the only character not taken from Austen's world, is a progressive man and a proto-feminist. As Mary is, he is a book nerd, and he is willing to give his wife her space, even travelling separate, such an indecorous act at the time. Therefore, while Mary will be, as her sisters are, provided for, she will maintain her independence. Gunderson and Melcon use Georgiana, Darcy's sister, to make the case for economic independence even clearer in the last play of the cycle. Georgiana is able to choose the husband she wants and gets free of her brother's guardianship because she does inherit money. In *Georgiana and Kitty*, she lives independently in London and, what is more, she 'pioneers women's rights' (Morin 2021). Together with Kitty, she founds the Society of Women Musicians, a metaphor for women's organizations that have struggled for women's self-definition and rights, and she challenges gender bias in the arts by revealing she has been writing music successfully under a male pen name. Even Lydia, the spoiled Bennet sister in Austen's work, earns her independence in Gunderson and Melcon's sequel. She unexpectedly divorces her infamous husband in the second play of the cycle, *The Wickhams*, a play that also stages working girls' independence through the character of

Cassie, a maid at Pemberley who refuses to marry just to be provided for. All in all, feminism in this Austen cycle shows the most acceptable face of the movement. The three plays are rich in popular feminist sentiments and pleasures. The spirit of romantic adventures is rewritten, as female characters' independence is not completely subjugated to heterosexual love. While some of the female characters find joy in traditional roles, others reject them and are erected as icons of female independence. Perhaps spectators are not interpellated as critics of patriarchy, but as joyous people who rejoice in feminism; being offered and sharing a respite from women's domestic lives and routines, leading spectators to think not only what we have, but to wonder what we might have.

The three plays in the cycle follow traditional and realistic formal patterns. Nevertheless, reviewing *Georgiana and Kitty*, non-professional, but prolific, critic Victor Cordell has identified a relation between its realistic staging and the play's feminism, an insight that is absent, however, from other professional reviews:

> the whole of the social contract comes under examination, some of which is stuck in time, but much of which bears relevance today. The impracticality of the ladies' costumes alone suggests the rigidity of the gender system which severely limits the activities of the women. These restrictions are compounded by notions of class and wealth distinctions; of propriety; family dynamics; the manner of meeting people; and arranged marriages, all of which inhibit women's mobility and freedom. (Cordell 2021)

Although other critics have not gone that far in identifying a feminist agenda in the mise-en-scène, there seems to be an agreement that the female characters defy 'corseted' gender expectations through their intelligence and humour (Feinsilber 2016, Jones 2016). The clearest agreement amongst critics, important for Gunderson's in-between feminism as seen so far, is the notion of sisterhood in all the three plays. Regardless of class and across familial bonds, women in these plays help one another to fulfil their dreams, both within the domestic and the artistic and labour domains. As Patricia L. Morin has said, 'Under the charm of the Bennet's family Christmas, Gunderson and Melcon remind us that powerful relationships help foster change, especially for women still burdened by patriarchal rules' (2021). *Miss Bennet*, *The Wickhams*, and *Georgiana and Kitty* provide stages for feminist hope in direct, non-experimental ways, and, as one critic has put it, the cycle 'makes a more appropriate holiday show than the kind of seasonal chestnut that draws more vaguely on nostalgia and the Christmas spirit' (Holman 2018). The popularity and success of the cycle promise holidays where sentimental feminism replaces Charles Dickens across stages in the United States.

Gunderson's turn to musicals is also concomitant with her understanding of feminist playwriting, in material and ideological ways. Gunderson has written a number of songs for her own plays, such as in *The Heath* or *The Revolutionists*, but her role in the writing of musicals is reduced to the libretto, 'to earning the songs' (Gunderson 2020d), and working closely with other artists. Her work for musicals is always in collaboration with other feminists. With Ari Afsar and Jordan Ealy for *Jeannette* (2020), with Joria Kwamé for 'Sinister', and with Kira Stone for 'Built for This'. Her collaborators for *Justice* (2020) are Bree Lowdermilk and Kait Kerrigan. The latter also collaborated with Gunderson in her only West End megamusical to date, *The Time Traveller's Wife* (2023), which also includes lyrics by pop star Dave Stewart and Joss Stone. Gunderson's intervention in the musical genre is recent but prolific. In 2020, she said that 'Musicals are the way to go because that's where the most money is spent in theatre' (in Pipino 2020). But such a financial reason is not her only motivation: 'The data tells us that when the stakes are really high, women aren't trusted as creators. And that when there's a lot of money, the opportunities continue to go to men. It's harder and harder for women to break into that. Women are way underrepresented when it comes to positions of power and money. But hopefully it is changing' (in Pipino 2020). Gunderson's musicals are thus political challenges to power and money positions, evidence that women can and should be behind what has been considered among the oldest, most popular, most profitable, most spectacular, and most recognizable forms of US culture (Wolf 2011). In doing so, she joins the incipient number of women playwrights collaborating in musicals in the States, from Marsha Norman's *The Color Purple* (2005), to Lynn Nottage's libretto for *MJ The Musical* (2021), to Sarah Ruhl's forthcoming adaptation of *The Interestings*. The intricacies of how Gunderson's collaborative musicals can be considered feminist interventions and how her works invite us to reimagine the possibilities of feminist musicals occupy this last section.

Almost from its very inception, the musical 'is reputedly deemed to be the most conservative' of all popular forms of entertainment (Aston 2013b:117). It has been considered a patriarchal form and, in many ways, antithetical to a feminist agenda. Firstly, musicals mainly reinforce heteronormativity. As Stacy Wolf has said, 'musical theatre's heteronormative conventions lodged long ago in the US cultural unconscious. Even musicals that buck the trend of the heterosexual couple formation . . . muse on love and heterosexual relationships' (2011: 8). Secondly, musicals have always favoured a fixed structure following linear development that ends in a happy ending. A defining quality of musicals is that they 'give us good feelings' (Wall 1996: 28); they are life-affirming at core: 'The sublime message of any musical show must ultimately be: life is worth it, even when things do not turn out all right in the end, the very existence of the artifact which is the show inspires hope, promotes growth, and re-affirms life' (Kislan 1995: 4–5). In Elaine Aston's words, 'The promise of the musical is that, entertaining us, it will make us feel better' (2013b: 117). This prioritizing of feelings over reason/intellect seems to devalue once again the potential feminist value of a given musical. Furthermore, in discussing this 'feel good' quality of musicals, Nathan Hurwitz has identified the common practice of 'preaching to the choir', that is, 'reaffirming the audience and making it feel good about itself' by stating something the audience already knew, 'like racism or bullying is bad' (2014: 244–245). Thus, the extent to which Gunderson and her collaborators' musicals depart from heteronormativity and how they transcend (or not) an emotional happy ending that reaffirms the audience and life in unquestioning ways seem the pivotal notions to discuss.

Following in the wake of the feminist musicals of the 1970s, which came to be erased by megamusicals in the 1980s (Wolf 2011: 128), Gunderson's musicals displace phallogocentrism. All her musicals are mainly populated by women. In some cases, male characters remain offstage or, when present, they are just secondary to the action. Gunderson's adaptation of *The Time Traveller's Wife* is an exception, and while its feminist potential is worth exploring, this romance-across-time megamusical is not the subject of my discussion. Resisting the traditional objectification of women bodies integral to patriarchal musicals (Wolf 2011: 52), it is in small-scale musicals, mainly staged at regional theatres that are liberated from the marketplace (Berkowitz 1996: 123), that Gunderson and her collaborators bring women centre stage as agents. And while romance is in the background of some of them, love – heterosexual and lesbian too – never monopolizes the action. The themes of these musicals remain as politically challenging as many of her plays.

'Built for This', Gunderson's ongoing project, workshopped under the auspices of the Olney Theatre's Vanguard Arts Fund and a recipient of an award by the Frank Young Fund for New Musicals in 2023, illustrates the ways in which feminist musicals can challenge patriarchy and traditional notions of the genre. The topic, far from the boy-meets-girl theme, brings onto the stage five young, talented women gymnasts in a scenario reminiscent of the years Larry Nashar abused the members of the US women national gymnastics team. Part fiction, part testimonial theatre, Gunderson intends to create entertainment, where these women's powerful bodies are celebrated, and at the same time denounces sexual abuse and the atmosphere of silence and denial the real survivors of this sexual predator went through. As typical of most of her works, and especially of her contributions to musicals, there is a call to resuscitate the notion of sisterhood. The national gymnastics team works as a metaphor for female bonding across class, race, and gender identity where women find support and a safe space from which to fight patriarchy. In doing so, Gunderson joins the latest trend in US musicals that offers 'inspiring and idealistic perspectives to its audiences ... that seek to project and embody qualities of courage, heroic resolve, and the capacity to do the right thing and overcome difficulties' (Knapp 2006: 164).

Gunderson's first feminist political musical remains a work in progress. *Jeannette*, which singer and song writer Ari Afsar had first imagined as a TV-movie, became a collaborative musical thanks to Gunderson's impetus. The play started its development at the O'Neill Theater Center's National Music Theater Conference in June 2019. COVID-19 pandemic hampered its live staging, but nonetheless it survived through staged readings and concerts till its production at 54Below in New York City in May 2023. The musical's breakout song, 'We Won't Sleep', inspired a 'Get out the Vote' video, and virtual performances of this song, by both Afsar and Gunderson, have been used for political purposes (Filichia 2021, Gunderson 2020a). *Jeannette* is a pop musical based on the true story of the US first congresswoman, Jeannette Rankin, a suffrage activist from Montana who was elected to Congress in 1916 – three years before the Nineteenth Amendment to the US Constitution granted women the right to vote. This musical joins the path initiated by second-wave feminists to bring centre stage and celebrate women lost to male-dominated versions of history, a path Gunderson walks in her historiographic pieces discussed in Section 2 of this Element. And as with others of Gunderson's plays, the approach is also overtly metatheatrical in order to show that history is in the making. The play opens with actresses demanding to know more about Jeannette Rankin, wondering, 'why we don't know who she is?' (2023a: 4). The first song, which typically situates the audience in the musical's world (Wolf 2011: 17), establishes Jeannete as 'our hero', a woman who lifted barriers for other women from within a very patriarchal system. After this first song, Gunderson verbalizes the aim of this musical: 'You've got to learn history before you make it' and 'You've got to get to the end of the story, before you start your own' (2023a: 5). In Gunderson's words, the theme 'is also about [Rankin's] legacy and people who've been excluded from power. It's this really cool dance of then-and-now, her-and-us' (in Filichia 2021). Mutual relations are established between history and story, past and present, Jeannete Rankin and spectators, as observed in key lines towards the end of the play: 'Learn from the past. Do better in the future' and 'our heroes need us ... not the other way around' (2023a: 93). The musical compels the audience to be active in rescuing the stories of women such as Rankin that have been lost to history; rescuing that story should lead to further action: one must 'learn from the past' to do 'better in the future'. The choice of Rankin as the protagonist is not free from polemics. As Erin Ortman, who directed the musical's version *Jeannette in Concert* at SubCulture New York, in 2019, has said, Rankin 'didn't win every fight and she didn't come out a national hero' (Ortman 2024). Significantly, Gunderson and her collaborators shun an idealized representation of this real woman to show both her political and human complexities. These complexities are also integral to the feminist movement itself since its beginning and, through *Jeannette*, we are invited to reconsider them so that we can do better in the future.

The play and its title character are based on a complex formal choice, atypical in musicals, that sustains the plot. The writers' feminist lens brings to the stage three different actresses in the role of Jeannette:

> JEANNETTE 1 – Black, political nerd, strategic, confident, wants to be the 'First'
> JEANNETTE 2 – White, activist, well meaning but blind, wants to 'change the world'
> JEANNETTE 3 – AAPI, queer, family-oriented, optimistic, loyal, wants to find 'belonging.' (2023a: 2)

This trinity allows creators to stage intersectional feminism, approaching the first feminist wave through this contemporary kind of feminism to signal blind spots in the history of feminism and still present in some contemporary feminist discourses. These three different voices, from their own perspectives, allow for a wide exploration of 'the very meaning of heroism, feminism, and activism' (Rabinowitz 2023). Having three women – one Black, on White, one queer AAPI – tell the story of Rankin is celebratory and questioning. The trio is used both to acknowledge that Rankin did open the path for all women to vote and access politics in the States and to realize her prioritization of the lives of white straight women. At the very beginning of the musical, Jeannette 3 remarks that Rankin was not only the first congresswoman in American history, but the 'First *queer* congresswoman in American History' (2023a: 3, emphasis in original). The political plot to have Jeannette elected has a running subplot about the relationship of Jeannette 3 with a Washington DC suffragist called Greenwich Martin. The romantic subplot, typical of musicals and only more recently involving lesbian and gay characters (Wolf 2018: 43), brings to surface the prejudices Rankin, as many other lesbians, had to face. Gunderson's Jeannette hides her homosexuality in her hometown, never reveals her true feelings to her family, and keeps her relationships secret. Eventually Jeannette 3 feels forced, especially by Jeannette 1 and Jeannette 2, to break up with Greenwich, a symbolic act understood as the pressures of heteronormative women on Rankin to maintain a profile that would make her more likeable, and which would be beneficial for the advancement of feminism at the time, or so they thought. Jeannette's political rise is met by her personal loss, which Jeannette 3 finds unacceptable, even more as her sexuality, her true identity, has been erased from history:

> JEANNETTE 3: You compromised *my* part of the story. I wanted a queer hero, someone I can look back to and say, 'she was out and she was loved and look at what she did!' For America, for women, yes, but also for *us, for queer people who were told we were wrong to love who we love, and we certainly weren't going to ever have the power she had, but she did.*
> JEANNETTE 2: Yes but I mean she never called herself gay, she never came out.
> JEANNETTE 3: Also she never married, lived with women her entire life, and sent pink frilly lingerie to very grateful ladies with whom she spent 'quality time'. That was not bestie behavior, she was gay.
> JEANNETTE 1: We don't know that for sure.
> JEANNETTE 3: *I do*. And I'm not telling this story without that part . . . You go and erase *my* part of the story, history's been doing that forever. Go ahead. Make a radical woman easier to sell. I won't do it! (2023a: 68, emphasis in original)

Gunderson and her colleagues make this point even clearer by having Jeannette 3 abandon the play, an embodiment of her refusal to be part of a false re-enactment of what Jeannette Rankin was for the sake of a straight pose some mainstream feminists would be happier with.

Disregarding her sexual interests and how she might have represented not only women but the queer community too is not the only compromise of Rankin that *Jeannette* brings to the stage. In a later scene, Jeannette 1 and Jeannette 2 meet with a Mississippi Congressman to win his sympathy for the Nineteenth Amendment. When he expresses his concern that this would mean giving black women the right to vote, Jeannette 2 does not hesitate to suggest: 'But couldn't you stop Black women from voting just like you already stop Black men?' (2023a: 88). The ensuing argument between both Jeannettes, with Jeannette 2 defining this compromise as a strategy to get the vote for all women later enacts the racial division between the feminist movement, which started then and would burgeon into the advance of the third wave. Symbolically, Jeannette 2 feels 'sorry' for having forced the abandonment of her feminist allies, an acknowledgement that first-wave white feminists monopolized the movement and fought mainly their own battles.

The apology, nevertheless, is not the end of the musical. Moving the audience close to that high-spirited feeling expected from musicals, the ending involves reconciliation and the belief that hope dwells in the fact that we 'Learn from the past [and can] Do better in the future' (2023a: 92). Stacy Wolf has noted that the last number, known as the '11 o'clock number', is 'especially memorable and resonant in terms of characterization, story, and emotional effect' (2011: 166). *Jeannette* ends with an ensemble number, in which all male and female characters in the play join, to underline the political refrain, 'We got to keep going /For the world that we are building' (2023a: 96). It is remarkable that during this last song, Gunderson writes, '*Jeannette 1, 2, and 3 do not come together. They are each still holding pain and betrayal. Through the song we come to know that they are not forgiven yet, but one day they might be. For now they will keep showing up, for the cause of equality and for each other. Which is all one person can really do*' (2023a: 94). This feminist musical is one that celebrates and provides an empowering representation of a key figure in US women's struggle for the right to vote. Its celebratory impetus, nonetheless, does not blur racial and sexual issues that remain important nowadays too. The feminist musical, Gunderson and her colleagues seem to say, should facilitate conversation among feminists so that the goals keep being fought for and won. In *Jeannette*, hope lies in learning from the mistakes of the past to amend the future, one where intersectional feminism walks ahead.

Gunderson also chooses to embody intersectional feminism through a trio in *Justice*, a musical that, however, is not as experimental (metatheatrical) in form as *Jeannette*. Gunderson became involved in this piece when Sean Daniel, artistic director of Arizona State Theatre, mused on a play about Sandra Day O'Connor, the first female justice of the US Supreme Court and a native from Arizona. Gunderson accepted the challenge but stipulated that Ruth Bader Ginsburg had to be in it as well. Eventually, the commission turned into a small-scale musical, running for 90 minutes, that explores the first three women on the US Supreme Court: Sandra Day O'Connor, Ruth Bader Ginsburg, and Sonia Sotomayor. The musical, primarily seen as a respectful homage to these three women (Encila-Celdran 2022, Jones 2023), is also feminist in practical ways as it is meant to provide an opportunity for actresses rarely seen nowadays. As Gunderson has said, 'What's really special about it, it's just three women, characters over 50, and you never see that in American theater' (in 'Intimate Look at 1st Women'). Linda Hodges, writing for Broadwayworld.com, has defined this musical as 'a herstory with a heart' (2023), an apt definition that involves some of Gunderson's defining theatrical traits: her revision of history through a feminist lens and the overt use of emotions.

Gunderson and her colleagues' revision of US contemporary political history proves highly educational, a quality pinpointed in most of the reviews (Reynolds 2023, Thomas 2023, Vega 2023). *Justice* makes evident these Justices' involvement in significant legal cases in the United States. These include landmark cases in feminist history, such as *Roe v. Wade*, the case that would allow US women to decide whether to continue with their pregnancies or terminate them and which was overturned in 2022. Gunderson and her collaborators' call for accuracy as regards these historical cases is evident in their request that 'words are visible somehow. The names of cases, the formal legal format of decisions, the 14th Amendment in its preciseness, The Constitution' (2023b: 2). Other cases brought onstage are *Mississippi v. Hogan* (on single-sex admission policy), *J.E.B. v. Alabama* (on a prospective juror's sex), *United States v. Virginia* (on the male-only admission policy of the Virginia Military Institute), and *Shelby County, Alabama v. The Attorney General of the United States Eric Holder* (on the constitutionality of two provisions of the Voting Rights Act of 1965). All these cases are pivotal in the execution of the Equal Protection Clause of the first section of the Fourteenth Amendment to the US Constitution that provides that 'nor shall any State . . . deny to any person within its jurisdiction the equal protection of the laws'. Equal justice, administered regardless of gender, race, class, or sexual choice, is at the core of these women's feminism that the play highlights.

Besides making use of projections and a literal approach to cases, the open didactic approach is also facilitated by a chronological order to the events. The action onstage covers from 1993, when Ruth Bader Ginsburg is in her new office at the US Supreme Court, till the present. A number of narrated and sung flashbacks are used to provide background information which aims to show the injustices these women had to fight before they came to their current positions of power. Despite graduating at the top of her class at Stanford, O'Connor did not get interviews and had to do volunteer work for a public defender (2023b: 6). And when she became a member of the Supreme Court, she was not even given a desk (2023b: 12). Similarly, Ginsburg, a brilliant student of Law at Harvard and Columbia, also suffered gender discrimination. She worked in the typing pool and was fired when she got pregnant, as this '*was not illegal* at that time' (2023b: 7, emphasis in original). Kelligan's lyrics explicitly expresses the gender bias these women had to fight: 'I have worked twice as hard / And twice as long,' sings Sandra, to be completed by Ruth's words: 'To prove that I'm worthy' (2023b: 9). Sonia Sotomayor's background is brought onstage by replicating parts of her speech at her Senate Confirmation Hearing, when she presented 'the progression of my life [... as] uniquely American'. A Puerto Rican who 'grew up in modest circumstances in a Bronx housing project' (2023b: 47), and who, through her own and her mother's efforts, attended Law School at Princeton, became a judge in the Southern District of New York, and the first Latina on the US Supreme Court. By introducing the audience to these women's pasts, the musical does not only establish these women as changemakers and trailblazers in US jurisprudence, but also makes spectators aware of these women's endurance as they fought their own injustices, and thus emerge as models to follow. The second song in the musical, 'New Justice', with a reprise in Act 2, explicitly brings together these women in singing 'Injustice for One /Is injustice for all' (2023b: 8), a line that summarizes the feminist zeal to build a more equalitarian world.

Justice makes explicit that for feminism to create a more equalitarian world women need to be in positions of power. Ruth Bader Ginsburg's famous line, that 'women belong in all the places decisions are made', is quoted in the play (2023b: 8), while the character of Sonia muses on the difference between powerful women and women with power: 'As a child, I knew a lot of powerful women in my life ... but not a lot of women with power. There were no women in law, no women mayors or police officers I ever saw' (2023b: 24). The relation between the label feminist and women's strategies to assume positions of power is brought to the stage as well. The character of Ruth confides to Sandra that she feels her self-description as 'a flaming feminist litigator' may be detrimental to her political purposes:

> RUTH: I don't know if they will ever accept me as anything but some feminist lawyer. How did you do it?
> SANDRA: By not being a feminist.
> RUTH: Sandra, you're the most powerful woman in America, you're a feminist whether you like it or not.
> SANDRA: I think I'll just be myself, how's that. (2023b: 19)

This conversation makes evident the still delicate issue of powerful women claiming feminism and the definition of feminism itself. As Gunderson herself has noted, 'Feminism doesn't need to be the thing that we name or wear on a shirt', Feminism is about 'making decisions towards equality and justice', 'living it, making it, being it is it' (2020b). The three women that populate *Justice* embody Gunderson's notion of Feminism.

As the three female characters that lead *Jeannette*, the description of the three female characters in *Justice* remarks their differences:

> SANDRA – White woman, 60
>> Headstrong, classy, by the book, no nonsense, a formidable and decisive leader. Everyone's big sister. Lawyer and former politician and elected official. Lover of spicy food. Wife and mother of three boys. Known to most as Sandra Day O'Connor, first woman Justice of the United States Supreme Court. White.
>
> RUTH – Jewish woman, 60
>> Calm, thoughtful, strategic. Enjoys a laugh, a good meal, a nice outfit, a moving opera. Defies assumptions of her firebrand personality by being generous, kind, and friend to all. Wife and mother of two as well as being a feminist activist and experienced judge, lawyer and professor. Known to most as Ruth Bader Ginsburg, second woman Justice of the United States Supreme Court. Jewish.
>
> SONIA – Puerto-Rican American woman, 50s
>> Diligent, level-headed, savvy and strong. Kind as well as fearless, she is not scared of being unflinchingly tough if the facts are behind her. Does not suffer fools. Fluent Spanish speaker, investigator, and rather a detective of the law. Diabetic, and early on dissuaded from being a lawyer because of it. Known to most as Sonia Sotomayor, first Latina on the Supreme Court. Puerto Rican-American. (2023b: 2)

The trio incorporates different ethnicities, origins, religions, manners, tastes, and personal stories. Their political differences are also brought to the stage. Sandra is 'a lifelong Republican and proud of it' (2023b: 33); her friendship with the Bushes and her role in the *Bush v. Gore* case, which would mark a breach between O'Connor and Ginsburg after the 2000 US Presidential election, are made manifest, in the same way that Ruth is depicted as a fervent Democrat. The political gap that has divided the United States since time immemorial is, nonetheless, here solved for feminist purposes. The bridge across these three characters' differences is their shared goal to fight for equality, and 'one extremely important quality: the courage to seek fairness for all – especially for those that often had for too long been disenfranchised in a male-dominated legal system' (Reynolds 2023). Such courage for a shared goal is what leads these women to provide support and encouragement in the play as apparently O'Connor, Ginsburg, and Sotomayor did in real life.

Typical of Gunderson's feminist dramaturgy explored so far, the notion of sisterhood is brought to the stage to remind women of the need to cooperate when a higher political goal is at stake. As the characters of Ruth and Sandra sing, theirs is 'An unlikely sisterhood/ We're hopelessly mismatched./ The red and blue of me and you/ Like stars and stripes all patched together' (2023b: 40–41). Oddities in a male-dominated world, these women help one another to navigate the intricacies of the Supreme Court, 'a minefield' where these women are always reminded that 'You are the 'woman"' (2023b: 22). Sandra comes to welcome Ruth on her first day of work at the Supreme Court offering her friendship and tips, the same way that Ruth welcomes Sonia and gives her a copy of her bench manual: 'Sandra did the same for me' (2023b: 53). Iconic forerunners show their most human face to provide support to other women. While the musical highlights the political importance of these three women, it succeeds even more in staging their humanity: 'Although these women have secured their place in history as icons of fairness and equality, *Justice: A New Musical* humanizes them in a way that somehow manages to make them even more iconic' (Thomas 2023). This sisterhood transcends the political sphere to turn into personal friendship. The most emotional scenes embody the most humane side of these women. Examples of empathy and support pervade the moments when Sandra tells of her husband's Alzheimer's disease – which leads her to leave the Supreme Court, when he dies, or when Sandra visits Ruth, after a nine-hour cancer surgery, and she advises on chemotherapy scheduling, based on her own experience, so that she can continue with her important work at the Supreme Court. Parts of O'Connor's letter to the United States on 23 October 2018, in which she publicly acknowledged she had started to suffer from dementia, are read by Sandra. These are lines her friends Ruth and Sonia underline and which express what had brought them together, despite their differences and their personal stories: 'I've seen first-hand how vital it is for all citizens to understand our Constitution and unique system of government – working collaboratively, putting country and common good above party and self-interest, and holding our key governmental institutions accountable' (2023b: 65). Sandra's farewell message encapsulates the engine of this sisterhood, which is hope; hope that through working together things can be changed.

Following the chronological development of the play, the ending takes place 'today', a present in need of feminist hope. News of other women appointed to the Supreme Court are mentioned and celebrated, especially the case of Ketanji Brown Jackson. Negative reviews of the play have pointed out the obvious absence of ultraconservative Amy Coney Barrett and Elena Kagan (Vega 2023, Willis 2023), claiming political bias on the part of Gunderson. Despite these reviews, most critics agree the trio formed by Sandra, Ruth, and Sonia works to foster that sense of ongoing hope for women to make the world fairer. Speaking in the present, Sonia acknowledges her forerunners' 'confirmations gave me something I desperately needed: Hope. I need that hope today. Right now' (2023b: 10). And the role of the three of them in the play is to provide hope to the audience. That by watching these women 'confront the battles of their time, [. . . the] audience is moved by the personal stories and perhaps motivated to step out and make a difference in social justice and equity in our own communities' (Wood in 'Trailblazing Musical' 2024). Other critics have also noted that the feeling of hope is not one to merely end with (Hodges 2023). As Sandra sings towards the end of the play, 'Hope is an endeavor' (2023b: 73). And thus, the musical has been seen as 'both a celebration of history and a militant call to arms' (Kruger 2023), a 'let's fight' final feminist call to hope for and work on a better future (Katz 2023). All in all, *Justice* ends on a happy note typical of musicals, perhaps a bit preachy though still necessary in calling the audience to 'dissent' and 'blaze' (2023b: 76), but, above all, one where a feminist utopianism seeps through the show's nostalgia for powerful and collaborative female political leaders. That the play has also been considered entertaining (Kruger 2023, Thomas 2023, Willis 2023) further provides hope for new feminist musicals that contribute to rewriting the common expectations of this genre.

As seen, Gunderson's contributions to shows usually considered mere entertainment prove their validity as a way to make feminist demands. These demands, as dramatized in the plays discussed in this section, include economic independence, the denunciation of gender abuse, the need for female political leaders and to have more women in positions of power, and the fight against racism and class prejudices. Gunderson's in-between feminism seems most obvious in these shows, above all as regards formal choices, where experimentation is generally secondary to didactic and direct approaches that celebrate and provide empowering representations of women. All in all, Gunderson's collaboration in romances and musicals and their general reception prove that feminist theatre makers can write entertaining works that are both pleasurable and profitable for their social value.

Conclusion

Back in 1995, in her influential *An Introduction to Feminism and Theatre*, Elaine Aston identified bourgeois feminism as having the aim 'to be accepted into the mainstream on mainstream (i.e., male) terms' (1995: 65). Lauren Gunderson's popularity might be misleading if we assume her feminism can be cast in this definition. Rather, I have contended in this Element that with her theatre, Gunderson invites us to reconsider the notion of Feminism and feminist theatre practice in the twenty-first century and urges today's 'feminist spectator in action' to cast her gaze expansively across the experimental, popular, feminist-political spectrum.

Throughout this Element, I have argued that Gunderson's feminist theatre is an 'in-between' practice, one that bridges past feminist practices and new directions, one that celebrates and demands more women's stories on the stage and which metamorphoses its tone, claims, and shapes to reach wide and varied audiences. Hers is a theatre that intervenes where and how the playwright feels a feminist lens is needed: from challenging Shakespeare and traditional conceptions of history, to contributing to innovative illness narratives and medical discourses, to expanding the possibilities of popular theatre forms such as musicals and romance. Gunderson's very varied works have proved to be ultimately provocative in challenging (hetero)sexist assumptions of white, heteropatriarchal discourses, and her innovations with form, whether through modified realism or more experimental practices, can be identified as clearly feminist, productive of new meaning and political at core. Her 'in-between' feminist theatre appears as a valuable tool to the contemporary feminist-theatre scene in the United States. While some may say that her works will not bring down the establishment directly, her theatre certainly inspires to learn and change.

As seen, Gunderson's multifaceted theatre practice does not represent a radical break with, or a rupturing of the feminist theatre tradition that grew out of the second wave; continuities can be found in the collaborative ethos of her women-centred theatre making and in the ongoing need to address social inequalities and injustices through theatre. It is then more a question of understanding how she renews that feminist tradition through the porosity of traditional and experimental forms. The keys to Gunderson's dramaturgy include populating the stage with female characters erected as models of empowerment within and outside their personal domains, and the overt use of emotions to draw the audience towards her protagonists. This is done in ways different from melodrama, and is politically driven so that her spectators' feelings for her protagonists compel them to react. A typical trait of Gunderson's dramaturgy, as seen in *The Revolutionists*, involves an appeal to the audience in the final moments of her plays to act against gender, class, and race injustices, and to collaborate in projecting a fairer world. Significantly, rather than ruling out 'man' as the target of feminist denunciations, as radical feminist practice would do in the past, Gunderson presents time and space as her protagonists' antagonists, a warning against continued heteropatriarchal conditions that still need to be fought. Gunderson's most clear debt to second-wave feminism, consistently presented in her works, is the notion of sisterhood, a notion problematic in itself for having disregarded intersectional feminism in the past in favour of white feminism. Gunderson integrates sisterhood and intersectional feminism successfully in many of her plays, as seen in *Justice* and *Jeannette*, for example. That theatre practice nowadays, and her works in particular, favour inclusive casting also invites us to reconsider the value that sisterhood, as presented in Gunderson's dramaturgy, might have nowadays for feminist purposes.

All in all, Gunderson's theatre adapts the legacies of second-wave feminist theatre to provide accessible experimental theatre and adopts popular genres in the interest of popular feminisms. In order to appreciate all this, there seems to be a need for modes of feminist criticism that, like Gunderson's theatre, can 'entertain' the idea of accessible experimental theatre and the use of popular forms for feminist ends. As seen throughout this Element, through parody, historiography, the Medical Humanities, romance and musicals, Gunderson's theatre provides the chance to picture new possibilities for women, past and present, and constitutes a hopeful stance for a more equalitarian society. Gunderson's works, as proposed by feminist gestic theory, allow us to examine and rethink class, gender, race, and ethnicity in proactive ways. As she says, 'we cannot manifest a better future until we start seeing it around us, until all of us see stories that not only reflect ourselves and the world we live in, but project a better world, a more inclusive and supportive world' (2024a: 505–506). Gunderson's popularity in the United States and its expansion worldwide are beneficial for a feminist theatre of hope. Her works challenge, educate, and feed back into the mainstream, enriching the contemporary stage through a still needed feminist lens.

References

Primary works by Lauren Gunderson: Plays and librettos

(nd). Earthrise. Manuscript
  Heart. Beat. Manuscript.
(2001). Midnight Bullfight. Manuscript.
(2003). Steel. Manuscript.
  Two Chairs: The Short Way to a Happy Ending. Manuscript.
  Two Pigeons Talk Politics. Manuscript.
(2004). Last Tape. Manuscript.
Sus Manos. Manuscript.
(2005). *Deepen the Mystery: Science and the South Onstage* (*Leap, Background, Parts They Call Deep*). Bloomington, IN: iUniverse.
  Mass. Manuscript.
(2006). *A Short History of Nearly Everything*. Manuscript.
(2007). The End of All Things. Manuscript.
(2008). Or Not. Manuscript.
(2009). *Emilie: La Marquise du Châtelet Defends Her Life Tonight*. New York: Samuel French.
(2011). *The Amazing Adventures of Dr. Wonderful and her Dog!* Manuscript.
(2012). By and By. Manuscript.
  Exit, Pursued by a Bear. New York: Playscripts Inc.
(2013). *Toil and Trouble*. New York: Playscripts, Inc.
  The Heath. Manuscript updated 2020.
(2014). *I and You. American Theatre Magazine* (July/August): 74–88. Rep. Methuen Modern Classics (2021a)
(2015). *Bauer*. New York: Dramatists Play Service.
  Damsel and Distress. Manuscript.
  Silent Sky. New York: Dramatists Play Service.
  The Taming. New York: Playscripts, Inc.
(2018). *Ada and the Engine*. New York: Dramatists Play Service.
  The Book of Will. New York: Dramatists Play Service.
  The Revolutionists. A Comedy. A Quartet. A Revolutionary Dream Fugue. A True Story. New York: Dramatists Play Service.
(2019). *Natural Shocks*. New York: Dramatists Play Service.
(2020). Trojan Women ATL. Manuscript.
(2021b). *The Catastrophist*. Torrazza Piemonte: Amazon Italia Logistica.

(2022). *The Half-Life of Marie Curie*. New York: Dramatists Play Service.

(2023). A Room in the Castle. Manuscript.

Artemisia. Manuscript.

Built for This. Libretto manuscript.

Jeannette. Libretto Manuscript. (2023a).

Justice. Libretto manuscript. (2023b).

Peter Pan and Wendy. A New Old Adventure. Manuscript.

Sinister. Libretto manuscript.

The Time Traveller's Wife. Libretto manuscript.

(2024). *Revolutionary Women. A Lauren Gunderson Play Collection*. Dubiner, Julie Felise, ed. London: Bloomsbury, Methuen Drama.

Gunderson, Lauren and Melcon, Margot (2017). *Miss Bennet: Christmas at Pemberley*. New York: Dramatists Play Service.

(2021). *The Wickhams: Christmas at Pemberley*. New York: Dramatists Play Service.

(2023). Georgiana and Kitty. Manuscript.

References: Secondary Sources

American Theatre Editors (2016). Lauren Gunderson's Inauguration Day Gift: A Free 'Taming'. *American Theatre*. 17 November. www.americantheatre.org/2016/11/17/lauren-gundersons-inauguration-day-gift-a-free-taming/.

Aston, Elaine (1995). *An Introduction to Feminism and Theatre*. London: Routledge.

(2013a). Jam and Jerusalem/Sentimentality and Feminism: *Calendar Girls*. In *A Good Night Out for the Girls: Performance Interventions*. London: Palgrave Macmillan, pp. 23–43.

(2013b). Work, Family, Romance and the Utopian Sensibilities of the Chick Megamusical *Mamma Mia!* In *A Good Night Out for the Girls: Performance Interventions*. London: Palgrave Macmillan, pp. 114–133.

(2016). Room for Realism? In Adisheshia, Siân, and LePage, Louise, eds. *Twenty-First Century Drama: What Happens Now*. Basingstoke: Palgrave Macmillan, pp. 17–35.

Aston, Elaine and Harris, Geraldine (2013). *A Good Night Out for the Girls: Popular Feminisms in Contemporary Theatre and Performance*. Basingstoke: Palgrave Macmillan.

Barthes, Roland (1972). *Critical Essays*, trans. Richard Miller. New York: Hill & Wang.

Billington, Michael (2018). Review I and You. *The Guardian*. 26 October. www.theguardian.com/stage/2018/oct/26/i-and-you-review-hampstead-theatre-london-game-of-thrones-maisie-williams.

Berkowitz, Gerald M. (1996). *New Broadways. Theatre Across America: Approaching a New Millennium*. New York: Applause.

Bleakley, A. (2013). Gender Matters in Medical Education. *Medical Education*, 47(1), 59–70.

  (2015). *Medical Humanities and Medical Education: How the Medical Humanities Can Shape Better Doctors*. London: Routledge.

Bloom, Harold (1994). *The Western Canon: The Books and School of the Ages*. New York: Riverhead Books.

Brall, Susan (2018). Review: 'Emilie: La Marquise du Châtelet Defends Her Life Tonight' at Silver Spring Stage. *DC Theatre Arts*. 16 September. https://dctheaterarts.org/2018/09/16/review-emilie-la-marquise-du-chatelet-defends-her-life-tonight-at-silver-spring-stage/.

Brady, Erik (2020). Opinion: Disney Plus needs to add some context to racist 'Peter Pan' now. *USA Today*. 18 July. https://eu.usatoday.com/story/opinion/2020/07/18/indigenous-peoples-peter-pan-nfl-washington-dc-racist-column/5453676002/.

Brantley, Ben (2016). Review: I and You is Lauren Gunderson's Sentimental Character Study. *New York Times*. 27 January. www.nytimes.com/2016/01/28/theater/review-i-and-you-is-lauren-gundersons-sentimental-character-study.html.

Brater, Enoch, ed. (1989) *Feminine Focus. The New Women Playwrights*. New York: Oxford University Press.

Brody, Howard (2011). Defining the Medical Humanities: Three Conceptions and Three Narratives. *Journal of Medical Humanities*, 32(1), 1–7.

Brodzinski, Emma (2016). Patient as Performer: Embodied Pathography in Contemporary Productions. In Mermikides, Alex and Bouchard, Gianna, eds., *Performance and the Medical Body*. London: Methuen Drama, pp. 85–97.

Burroughs, Catherine and Gainor, J. Ellen, eds. (2024). *Routledge Anthology of Women's Theatre Theory and Criticism*. London: Routledge.

Callaghan, Dympna (1999). *Shakespeare Without Women*. Hoboken, NJ: Taylor & Francis Group.

Canning, Charlotte (1996). *Feminist Theatres in the U.S.A.: Staging Women's Experience*. London: Routledge.

  (2004). Feminist Performance as Feminist Historiography. *Theatre Survey*, 45(2), 227–233.

Carlson, Marvin (2011). *The Haunted Stage: The Theatre as Memory Machine*. Ann Arbor: University of Michigan Press.

Case, Sue-Ellen (1988). *Feminism and Theatre*. New York: Methuen.

Chansky, Dorothy (2023). *Losing It: Staging the Cultural Conundrum of Dementia and Decline in American Theatre*. Cham, Switzerland: Palgrave Macmillan.

Chinoy, Helen Krich and Jenkins, Linda Walsh (1987). *Women in American Theatre*. New York: Theatre Communication Group.

Clay, Carolyn (2017). Sisterhood Meets The Guillotine In 'The Revolutionists' At Central Square Theater. Wbur.org. 25 October. www.wbur.org/news/2017/10/25/the-revolutionists-central-square-review.

Coddon, David L. (2022). Review: 'The Taming' a Fragile Mix of Pageantry, Power Play and Politics. *San Diego Union Tribune*. 18 April. www.sandiegouniontribune.com/entertainment/theater/story/2022-04-18/review-the-taming-a-fragile-mix-of-pageantry-power-play-and-politics.

Cohen, Laura Foti (2023). Theatre Review: The Revolutionists. Larchmont Village Life Theatre. 23 May. https://larchmontbuzz.com/larchmont-village-life/theater-review-the-revolutionists/.

Collins-Hughes, Laure (2018). Review: In 'Natural Shocks,' a Storm Is Coming. *New York Times*. 9 November. www.nytimes.com/2K018/11/09/theater/natural-shocks-review.html.

Cordell, Victor (2021). Georgiana & Kitty: Christmas at Pemberley. Cordell Reports. 26 November. https://cordellreports.com/2021/11/26/georgiana-kitty-christmas-at-pemberley/.

Cott, Nancy F. (1972). *Roots of Bitterness: Documents of the Social History of American Women*. New York: E. P. Dutton.

Couser, G. Thomas (1997). *Recovering Bodies. Illness, Disability, and Life Writing*. Madison: University of Wisconsin Press.

Dallas, Toni (2016). The Revolutionists. *Toni Dallas Theatre Reviews*. https://tonydallastheatrereviews.blogspot.com/2016/02/the-revolutionists.html.

Dash, Irene (1981). *Wooing, Wedding, and Power: Women in Shakespeare's Plays*. New York: Columbia University Press.

David, Jacob (2017). Review of Silent Sky. Around the town. https://aroundthetownchicago.com/theatre-reviews/silent-sky-reviewed-by-jacob-davis/.

Derr, Holly L. (2022). Recognition and Reversal in the Plays of Lauren Gunderson: A Dialogue with the Playwright. *Journal of Dramatic Theory and Criticism*, 36(2),73–84.

Desmet, Christy (2014). Recognizing Shakespeare, Rethinking Fidelity: A Rhetoric and Ethics of Appropriation. In Huang, Alexa and Rivlin,

Elizabeth, eds., *Shakespeare and the Ethics of Appropriation*. New York: Palgrave Macmillan, pp. 41–57.

Diamond, Elin (1997). *Unmaking Mimesis: Essays on Feminism and Theatre*. London: Routledge.

Dickinson, Nerida (2021). Review I and You. Artshub. 31 May. www.artshub.com.au/news/reviews/theatre-review-i-and-you-262690-2371145/.

Dolan, Jill (2013). *The Feminist Spectator in Action. Feminist Criticism for the Stage and Screen*. New York: Palgrave Macmillan.

Dubiner, Julie Felise (2024). Introduction. In *Revolutionary Women: A Lauren Gunderson Play Collection*. London: Bloomsbury, Methuen Drama, pp. 1–7.

Dusinberre, Juliet (1975). *Shakespeare and the Nature of Women*. London: Macmillan.

Edson, Margaret and Gunderson, Lauren (2014). Southern Hospitality: An Interview with the Playwright. *American Theatre Magazine* (July/August), 72–73.

Elam, Jr., Harry J. (2010). The High Stakes of Identity: Lorraine Hansberry's *Follow the Drinking Gourd* and Suzan-Lori Parks's *Venus*. In Postlewait, Thomas and Canning, Charlotte M., eds., *Representing the Past: Essays in Performance Historiography*. Iowa: University of Iowa Press, pp. 282–302.

Ell, Jenny (2021). Review: The Catastrophist, Marin Theatre Company & Round House Theatre. West End Best Friend. 28 January. www.westendbestfriend.co.uk/news/review-the-catastrophist-marin-theatre-company-and-round-house-theatre.

Encila-Celdran, Robert (2022). Review: JUSTICE Gets It Done Where Decisions Are Made. Broadwayworld.com. 19 April. www.broadwayworld.com/phoenix/article/BWW-Review-JUSTICE-Gets-It-Done-Where-Decisions-Are-Made-20220419.

Faiella, Betsyann (2023). Review of Emilie: La Marquise du Châtelet Defends Her Life Tonight. Front Row Center. 13 April. https://thefrontrowcenter.com/2023/04/emilie-la-marquise-du-chatelet-defends-her-life-tonight/.

Falkenstein, Linda (2023). An Artist Breaks Free in Forward Theater's 'Artemesia'. *Isthmus*. 15 April. https://isthmus.com/arts/stage/artist-breaks-free-in-artemesia-madison-forward-theater/.

Farmer, Tina (2016). 'Exit, Pursued by a Bear' is a Tale of Love and Vengeance Delivered with a Comic Twist. *KDHX*. https://kdhx.org/articles/theatre-reviews/1469-exit,-pursued-by-a-bear%E2%80%99-is-a-tale-of-love-and-vengeance-delivered-with-a-comic-twist.

Feinsilber, Pamela (2016). The Timely Joys of Miss Bennet: Christmas at Pemberley. HuffPost. 1 December. www.huffpost.com/entry/the-timely-joys-of-miss-b_b_13359706.

Feng, Rhoda (2023): Emilie' Review: Defending, and Defining, a Life. *New York Times*. 18 April. www.nytimes.com/2023/04/18/theater/emilie-du-chatelet-review.html.

Fetterly, Judith Fetterly (1978). *The Resisting Reader.* Bloomington: Indiana University Press.

Filichia, Peter (2021). Lauren Gunderson Meets Jeannette Rankin. Official Masterworks Broadway Site. 23 March. www.masterworksbroadway.com/blog/lauren-gunderson-meets-jeannette-rankin-by-peter-filichia/.

Fischer, Mike (2023). Who Lives, Who Dies, Who Tells Her Story? – Lauren Gunderson's ARTEMISIA Takes Control of the Narrative. World Premiere Wisconsin. 7 April. https://worldpremierewisconsin.com/who-lives-who-dies-who-tells-her-story/.

Folliard, Patrick (2023). 'A Room in the Castle' Highlights the Women of 'Hamlet.' *Washington Blade*. 15 January. www.washingtonblade.com/2023/01/15/a-room-in-the-castle-highlights-the-women-of-hamlet/.

Foster, Sherri L. and Funke, Jana (2018). Introduction: Feminist Encounters with the Medical Humanities. *Feminist Encounters: A Journal of Critical Studies in Culture and Politics*, 2(2), 1–6.

Fricker, Karen and MacArthur, Michelle (2024). The Emancipated Amateur: Rancierian Reviewing Practices and New Models of Theatre Criticism. *Theatre Research in Canada*, 45(1), 11–29.

Friedman, Sharon (2009). *Feminist Theatrical Revisions of Classic Works: Critical Essays*. Jefferson: McFarland.

Gainor, J. Ellen, Garner, Stanton, B. Jr., and Puchner, Martin, eds. (2009). *Norton Anthology of Drama*. New York: W.W. Norton.

Garner, Stanton B. Jr. (2020). Bodies of Knowledge: Theatre and Medical Science. In Shepherd-Barr, Kirsten, ed., *The Cambridge Companion to Theatre and Science*. Cambridge: Cambridge University Press, pp. 85–100.

  (2023). *Theatre & Medicine*. London: Methuen.

Gilbert, Sandra M. and Gubar, Susan (1979). *The Madwoman in the Attic: The Woman Writer and the Nineteenth-Century Literary Imagination*. New Haven: Yale University Press.

  eds. (1985). *Norton Anthology of Literature by Women*. New York: W.W. Norton.

  (2021). *Still Mad. American Women Writers and the Feminist Imagination*. New York: W.W. Norton.

Glyer, Mike (2019). Peter Pan and Wendy. File 770. 5 December. https://file770.com/peter-pan-and-wendy/.

Green, Jesse (2016). Theater Review: I and You and a Plot Twist, Too. Vulture. 27 January. www.vulture.com/2016/01/theater-review-i-and-you.html.

(2021). Review: Playwriting and Bug-Hunting Wed in 'The Catastrophist.' *The New York Times*. 23 February. www.nytimes.com/2021/01/28/theater/the-catastrophist-review.html.

Grogan, Nathalie (2021). 'The Catastrophist' is self-aware storytelling of a virus hunter's life. *Daily Californian*. 1 February. www.dailycal.org/archives/the-catastrophist-is-self-aware-storytelling-of-a-virus-hunter-s-life/article_7851fbe2-bac6-5654-8d26-8a4c80baa3d5.html.

Gunderson, Lauren (nd). The Revolutionists: Dramaturgy. https://therevolutionists.tumblr.com/.

(2013). We Are Not a Mirror Theatre Must Lead with Women's Stories. HowlRound Theatre Commons. 24 April. https://howlround.com/we-are-not-mirror.

(2015). Survival of the Storied: Why Science Needs Art and Art Needs Science. Manuscript.

(2016). Write Like Jane! Marin Theatre Company website. www.marintheatre.org/press-release-details/98/write-like-jane.

(2017) The Book of Will – Lauren Gunderson. Podcast. Shakespeare Unlimited. Folger Library Website. 5 April. www.folger.edu/podcasts/shakespeare-unlimited/the-book-of-will/.

(2020a). Arts + Activism: Jeannette & Making Political Musical Theatre – Lauren Gunderson on Thurs 6 Aug 2020. YouTube. HowlRound Theatre Channel. 6 August. www.youtube.com/watch?v=8qDDvHxbkMo&t=3s.

(2020b). Feminism + Theatre with Marissa Wolf, Hana Sharif, and Ari Afsar. Lauren Gunderson Facebook Page. www.facebook.com/100063477763274/videos/675539279892249/?__so__=watchlist&__rv__=video_home_www_playlist_video_list.

(2020c). Lauren Gunderson: Playwright. Podcast. National Endowment for the Arts, 6 March. www.arts.gov/stories/podcast/lauren-gunderson.

(2020d). Musical Theatre Writing w/ Lauren + Kait Kerrigan + Bree Lowdermilk. Lauren Gunderson Facebook Page, 10 April. www.facebook.com/100063477763274/videos/709653856442100/?__so__=watchlist&__rv__=video_home_www_playlist_video_list.

(2020e). Playwriting Class Part 2. Lauren Gunderson Facebook Page. 25 March. www.facebook.com/LaurenGundersonPlaywright/videos/playwriting-class-part-2/261185331579926.

(2020f). Playwriting Class 3. Emotion, Conflict, Theatricality, 1 Person Shows. Lauren Gunderson Facebook Page. 11 April. www.facebook.com/LaurenGundersonPlaywright/videos/playwriting-class-3-emotion-conflict-theatricality-1-person-shows/207482510690035.

(2024a). Excerpt from 'Survival of the Storied: Why Science Needs Art and Art Needs Science'. In Burroughs, Catherine and Gainor, J. Ellen, eds., *Routledge Anthology of Women's Theatre Theory and Criticism*. London: Routledge, pp. 504–509.

(2024b). Lauren Gunderson on William Shakespeare. Recorded talk. Modern Drama Seminar. Chair Noelia Hernando-Real. Universidad Autónoma de Madrid.

(2024c). Preface. In Julie Felise Dubiner, ed., *Revolutionary Women: A Lauren Gunderson Play Collection*. Ed. Julie Felise Dubiner. London: Bloomsbury, Methuen Drama, pp. vii–viii.

Hall, Kim F. (1996). *Things of Darkness: Economies of Race and Gender in Early Modern England*. Ithaca, NY: Cornell University Press.

Harris, Amita W. (2023). Review: Smart, Funny and Poignant 'The Book of Will' at A Noise Within. LA Theatrix. 18 May. www.latheatrix.com/post/review-smart-funny-and-poignant-the-book-of-will-at-a-noise-within.

Hart, Lynda, ed. (1989). *Making a Spectacle: Feminist Essays on Contemporary Women's Theatre*. Ann Arbor: University of Michigan Press.

Hawkins, Anne Hunsaker (1999). Pathography: Patient Narrative of Illness. *Culture and Medicine*, 171, 128.

Hertvik, Nicole (2019). Playwright Lauren Gunderson had one stipulation when reworking 'Peter Pan'. The sexism and racism had to go. *DC Theatre Arts*. 2 December. https://dctheaterarts.org/2019/12/02/lauren-gunderson-peter-pan-and-wendy/.

Higgins, Molly (2025). Folger Theatre Will Stage the World Premiere of Lauren M. Gunderson's A Room in the Castle. Playbill. Playbill.com. 15 February. https://playbill.com/article/folger-theatre-will-stage-the-world-premiere-of-lauren-m-gundersons-a-room-in-the-castle.

Hodges, Linda (2023). Review: JUSTICE: A NEW MUSICAL at Marin Theatre Company. Broadway World. Com. 6 March. www.broadwayworld.com/san-francisco/article/Review-JUSTICE-A-NEW-MUSICAL-at-Marin-Theatre-Company-20230306.

Holledge, Julie (1981). *Innocent Flowers: Women in the Edwardian Theatre*. London: Virago.

Holman, Curt (2018). Review: Theatrical Outfit's 'Miss Bennet' Brings Holiday Cheer to Jane Austen Sequel. ARTSATL. 18 November. www.artsatl.org/review-theatrical-outfits-miss-bennet-brings-holiday-cheer-to-jane-austen-sequel/#:~:text=Ultimately%20the%20play%20finds%20considerable,of%20love%2C%20marriage%20and%20sisterhood.

Howey, Christine (2023). 'Exit, Pursued by a Bear' at Convergence-Continuum Lacks Almost Everything. *Scene*. 14 August. www.clevescene.com/arts/exit-pursued-by-a-bear-at-convergence-continuum-lacks-almost-everything-42554588.

Huang, Alexa and Rivlin, Elizabeth (2014). Introduction. In Alexa Huang and Elizabeth Rivlin, eds., *Shakespeare and the Ethics of Appropriation*. New York: Palgrave Macmillan, pp. 1–20.

Hurwitt, Robert (2011). 'Exit, Pursued by a Bear' Review: Funny and Quick. *SFGate*. 25 August. www.sfgate.com/performance/article/Exit-Pursued-by-a-Bear-review-funny-and-quick-2333860.php.

(2013). 'Taming' Review: Beauty Queen Takes Political Prisoners. *SFGate*. 9 October. www.sfgate.com/performance/article/Taming-review-Beauty-queen-takes-political-4882694.php.

Hurwitz, Nathan (2014). *A History of the American Musical Theatre: No Business Like It*. New York: Routledge.

Hutcheon, Linda (2000). *A Theory of Parody. The Teachings of Twentieth-century Art Forms*. New York: Methuen.

Intimate Look at 1st Women on U.S. Supreme Court in 'JUSTICE: A New Musical'. *CBS News Bay Area*. February 2023. www.cbsnews.com/sanfrancisco/news/justice-a-new-musical-1st-women-on-u-s-supreme-court/.

Janiak, Lily (2016). Marin's 'Miss Bennet' a New Christmas Classic. *San Francisco Chronicle*. 30 November. www.sfchronicle.com/performance/article/MTC-s-Miss-Bennet-a-new-Christmas-classic-10645158.php.

Jays, David (2023). The Book of Will Review – Friends Fight to Save Shakespeare's Plays. *The Guardian*. 3 May. www.theguardian.com/stage/2023/may/03/the-book-of-will-review-queens-theatre-hornchurch.

Jones, Chad (2016). Lost in Austen with Marin's Christmas at Pemberly. Chad Jones's Theater Dogs. 29 November. www.theaterdogs.net/reviews/2016/11/30/lost-in-austen-with-marins-christmas-at-pemberly.

(2023). At Marin Theatre Company, these Supremes sing of Justice. Chad Jones's Theatre Dogs. 22 February. www.theaterdogs.net/reviews/2023/02/22/at-marin-theatre-company-justice-sings.

Jones, Chris (2012). Review Exit, Pursued by a Bear. Theatre in Chicago. www.theatreinchicago.com/exit-pursued-by-a-bear/reviews/5552/.

Karim-Cooper, Farah (2023). *The Great White Bard*. New York: Penguin.

Katz, Leslie (2023). Review: Marin Theatre's 'Justice' Tells Thrilling Stories Of Supreme Court Heroines. *SF Gate*. 23 February. www.sfgate.com/news/bayarea/article/review-marin-theatre-s-justice-tells-17802478.php.

Kelly, Katherine E. (2020). Making the Bones Sing: The Feminist History Play, 1976-2010. *Theatre Journal*, 62(4), 645–660.

Kemper, Ben (2017). Review of Silent Sky. *Chicago Theatre Review*. Theatre in Chicago. www.theatreinchicago.com/silent-sky/reviews/9100/.

Kislan, Richard (1995). *The Musical: A Look at the American Musical Theater*. New York: Applause.

Kleinman, A. (1980). *Patients and Healers in the Context of Culture*. Berkeley: University of California Press.

(1986). *Social Origins of Distress and Disease*. New Haven: Yale University Press.

Knapp, Raymond (2006). *The American Musical and the Performance of Personal Identity*. Princeton: Princeton University Press.

Kneebone, Roger (2016). Performing Surgery. In Mermikides, Alex and Bouchard, Gianna, eds., *Performance and the Medical Body*. London: Methuen Drama, pp. 67–82.

Kolodny, Annette (1975). *The Lay of the Land: Metaphor as Experience in American Life and Letters*. Chapel Hill: University of North Carolina Press.

Korda, Natasha (2011). *Labors Lost: Women's Work and the Early Modern English Stage*. Philadelphia: University of Pennsylvania Press.

Kruger, Charles (2023). Review of Justice at Marin Theatre Company. Theatre Storm. 7 March. https://theatrestorm.com/2023/03/07/review-justice-world-premiere-musical-at-marin-theatre-company-last-chance-closes-this-weekend/.

Lanier, Douglas (2014). Shakespearean Rhizomatics: Adaptation, Ethics, Value. In Huang, Alexa and Rivlin, Elizabeth, eds., *Shakespeare and the Ethics of Appropriation*. New York: Palgrave Macmillan, pp. 21–40.

Launer, Pat (2022). Women Gone Wild ... and Political ... in 'The Taming' at Scripps Ranch Theatre. *Times of San Diego*. 20 April. https://timesofsandiego.com/arts/2022/04/20/women-gone-wild-and-political-in-the-taming-at-scripps-ranch-theatre/.

Lefty, Lucy (2023). Review Exit, Pursued by a Bear. *Out All Day: New Orleans*. 6 April. www.outalldaynola.com/news/review-exit-pursued-by-a-bear.

Lenz, Carol Ruth Swift, Greene, Gayle and Thomas, Carol, eds. (1980). *The Woman's Part: Feminist Criticism of Shakespeare*. Urbana: University of Illinois Press.

Little, Jr, Arthur L. (2022). *White People in Shakespeare: Essays on Race, Culture and the Elite*. London: Bloomsbury.

Loomba, Ania, and Orkin, Martin. (1998). *Post-Colonial Shakespeares*. Hoboken, NJ: Taylor and Francis.

Lyman, David (2016). Review: 'The Revolutionists' Has Beheading, Lots of Laughs. Cincinnati.com. https://eu.cincinnati.com/story/entertainment/the

ater/2016/02/12/review-revolutionists-has-beheading-lots-laughs/80303254/.

Mandell, Jonathan (2016). I and You Review. DC Theatre Scene. 27 January. https://dctheatrescene.com/2016/01/27/i-and-you-review-teenagers-facing-life-and-death-through-walt-whitman/.

Marks, Peter (2021). A New Play Mints a New Dramatic Star for Our Time: A Virologist. *Washington Post*. 30 January. www.washingtonpost.com/coronavirus/round-house-theatre-the-catastrophist-review/2021/01/30/72e9c53c-6315-11eb-9430-e7c77b5b0297_story.html.

McConachie, Bruce (2020). Reenacting Events to Narrate Theatre History. In Postlewait, Thomas and Canning, Charlotte M., eds., *Representing the Past: Essays in Performance Historiography*. Iowa: University of Iowa Press, pp. 378–403.

Mermikides, Alex and Bouchard, Gianna (2016). Introduction. In Alex Mermikides and Gianna Bouchard, eds., *Performance and the Medical Body*. London: Methuen Drama, pp. 1–20.

Morin, Patricia L. (2021). 'Georgiana and Kitty: Christmas at Pemberley' Pioneers Woman's Rights- at MTC. Theatrius. 30 November. https://theatrius.com/2021/11/30/georgiana-kitty-christmas-at-pemberley-pioneers-womens-rights-at-mtc/.

Onofri, Adrienne (2023). Review of Emilie. *Off Off Online*. www.offoffonline.com/offoffonline/2023/4/10/emilie-la-marquise-du-chtelet-defends-her-life-tonight.

Ortman, Erin (2024). Jeannette. Erinnortman.com. https://erinortman.com/jeannette/.

Our Bodies Ourselves Today. The History & Legacy of Our Bodies Ourselves. Our Bodies Ourselves Today. www.ourbodiesourselves.org/about-us/our-history/.

Paine, Herbert (2021). Review: Lauren Gunderson's THE HEATH at Arizona Theatre Company Is A Masterpiece That Must Be Heard To Be Seen. 14 April. Broadwayworld Arizona. www.broadwayworld.com/phoenix/article/BWW-Review-Lauren-Gundersons-THE-HEATH-at-Arizona-Theatre-Company-Is-A-Masterpiece-That-Must-Be-Heard-To-Be-Seen-20210414.

Paterson, Eddie (2015). *The Contemporary American Monologue: Performance and Politics*. London: Bloomsbury.

Pipino, Kiara. (2020). Lauren Gunderson. In *Women Writing and Directing in the USA: A Stage of Our Own*. New York and London: Routledge. Online.

Pressley, Nelson (2014). Lauren Gunderson's 'I and You' is a Crafty Drama that Mostly Escapes Sentimentality. *Washington Post*. 7 March. www.washing

tonpost.com/entertainment/theater_dance/lauren-gundersons-i-and-you-is-a-crafty-drama-that-mostly-escapes-sentimentality/2014/03/07/e7ec38f0-a61c-11e3-a5fa-55f0c77bf39c_story.html.

Q&A: Playwright Lauren Gunderson (2019). Merrimack Repertory Theatre Blog. https://mrt.org/blog-item/qa-playwright-lauren-gunderson.

Rabinowitz, Chloe (2023). Ari Afsar, Asmeret Ghebremichael & More to Star in JEANETTE: THE MUSICAL at 54 Below. Broadway World.com. 20 April. www.broadwayworld.com/cabaret/article/Ari-Afsar-Asmeret-Ghebremichael-More-to-Star-in-JEANETTE-THE-MUSICAL-at-54-Below-2023%E2%80%A6.

Radosavljević, Duška, ed. (2016). *Theatre Criticism: Changing Landscapes*. London: Bloomsbury Methuen Drama.

Rebell, Sarah (2018). Natural Shocks: An Interview with Lauren Gunderson, May Adrales and Pascale Armand. *The Interval*. 8 November. www.theintervalny.com/interviews/2018/11/natural-shocks-an-interview-with-lauren-gunderson-may-adrales-and-pascale-armand/.

Reyes, Natalie (2012). Impact's Newest Plays on Shakespeare, Entrepreneurship. *Daily Californian*. 15 November. www.dailycal.org/2012/11/15/impacts-newest-plays-on-shakespeare-entrepreneurship.

Reynolds, Eddie (2023). Justice: A New Musical. Theatre Eddys. San Francisco Bay Area Theatre Reviews. 23 February. https://theatreeddys.com/2023/02/justice-a-new-musical.html.

Robinson, Lillian S. (1983). Treason Our Text: Feminist Challenges to the Literary Canon. *Tulsa Studies in Women's Literature*, 2(1), 83–98.

Robinson, Alice M., Roberts, Vera Mowray and Barran, Milly S. (1989). *Notable Women in American Theatre: A Biographical Dictionary*. Westport, CO: Greenwood.

Rose, Margaret (1979). *Parody/Metafiction*. London: Croomhell.

Rutter, Carol Chillington (2001). *Enter the Body: Women and Representation on Shakespeare's Stage*. Hoboken, NJ: Taylor & Francis Group.

Schlueter, June, ed. (1991). *Modern American Drama: The Female Canon*. London: Associated University Presses.

Scott, Joan (1988). *Gender and the Politics of History*. New York: Columbia University Press.

SF Bay Guardian (2012). Review of 'Toil and Trouble'. 20 November.

Shai, Ayelet, Sahar Koffler and Yael Hashiloni-Dolev (2021). Feminism, Gender Medicine and Beyond: A Feminist Analysis of 'Gender Medicine'. *International Journal of Equity in Health*, 20(177), 1–11.

Shakespeare and Beyond (2023). Q&A: Lauren Gunderson on her New Play, A Room in the Castle, about the Women of Hamlet. Folger Shakespeare

Library. 3 January. www.folger.edu/blogs/shakespeare-and-beyond/qa-lauren-gunderson-new-play-a-room-in-the-castle-reading-room/.

Sharma, Malika (2019). Applying Feminist Theory to Medical Education. *The Lancet*, 393, 570–578.

Shepherd-Barr, Kirsten (2006). *Science on Stage: From Doctor Faustus to Copenhagen*. Princeton: Princeton University Press.

Showalter, Elaine (1977). *A Literature of Their Own*. Princeton: Princeton University Press.

Shurley, Neil (2020). Review: Lauren Gunderson's The Heath Creates Theatre Magic at Warehouse Theatre. 25 January. Broadwayworld South Carolina. www.broadwayworld.com/south-carolina/article/BWW-Review-Lauren-Gundersons-THE-HEATH-Creates-Theatre-Magic-at-Warehouse-Theatre-20200125.

Smith, Kelundra (2016). Review: Playwright Lauren Gunderson Reframes 'Herstory' in 'The Revolutionists' at 7 Stages. *ARTSATL*. 15 March. www.artsatl.org/review-playwright-lauren-gunderson-revolutionists-7-stages/.

Smith, Susan Harris (1997). *American Drama: The Bastard Art*. New York: Cambridge University Press.

Snook, Ravel (2019). Review of The Half Life of Marie Curie. *Time Out New York*. 19 November. www.timeout.com/newyork/theater/the-half-life-of-marie-curie.

Sochen, June (1974). *Herstory: A Woman's View of American History*. New York: Alfred Publishing.

Solga, Kim (2016). *Theatre & Feminism*. New York: Palgrave Macmillan. Online.

  (2024). *Women Making Shakespeare in the Twenty-First Century*. Cambridge: Cambridge University Press (Elements in Women Theatre Makers).

Sontag, Susan (1978). *Illness as Metaphor*. London: Picador.

Southbank Theatre (2022). Audience Members React to Natural Shocks. YouTube. November. www.youtube.com/watch?app=desktop&v=WHNDSUAYJ0A.

Speak Up and Speak Out: Audience Reactions to Natural Shocks. (2018). YouTube. Fountain Theatre channel. April 2028. www.youtube.com/watch?v=sDYUGVBmhoU.

Teachman, Eric (2017). Capital Fringe Review: 'Exit, Pursued by a Bear' at Barabbas Theatre. 10 July. *DC Theater Arts*. https://dctheaterarts.org/2017/07/10/2017-capital-fringe-review-exit-pursued-bear-barabbas-theatre/.

Thomas, Patrick (2023). Review of Justice: A New Musical. Marin Theatre Company. Talking Broadway. www.talkinbroadway.com/page/regional/sanfran/s2137.html.

Thompson, Ayanna, ed. (2021). *The Cambridge Companion to Shakespeare and Race*. Cambridge University Press.

Trailblazing Musical Comes to Whidbey Island Center for the Arts (2023). Whidbey Island Arts Center. 8 April. www.wicaonline.org/blog/2024/4/9/trailblazing-musical-justice-comes-to-whidbey-island-center-for-the-arts.

Tresca, Toni (2022). Confusing Script Undermines 'The Revolutionists.' *Onstage Colorado*. 20 September. https://onstagecolorado.com/confusing-script-undermines-the-revolutionists/.

Vaughan, Megan (2020). *Theatre Blogging: The Emergence of a Critical Culture*. London: Methuen Drama.

Vega, Beulah (2023). Jury's Out on 'Justice: A New Musical'. *Pacific Sun*. 28 February. https://pacificsun.com/jurys-out-on-justice-a-new-musical/.

Velasco, Dorothy (2018). Ashland Theater Review: The Book of Will. *KLCC*. July 17. www.klcc.org/arts-culture/2018-07-17/ashland-theater-review-the-book-of-will.

Wall, Carey (1996). There's No Business Like Show Business: A Speculative Reading of the Broadway Musical. In Lawson-Peebles, Robert, ed., *Approaches to the American Musical*. Exeter: Exeter University Press, pp. 24–43.

Weinert-Kendt, Rob (2017). Criticism Needs Support (and a Diversity Upgrade). *American Theatre*. 13 April. www.americantheatre.org/2017/04/13/criticism-needs-support-and-a-diversity-upgrade/.

Wiesler, Russell H. (2014). Evolving Trends in Liver Transplantation Listing and Liver Donor Allocation. *Clinics in Liver Disease*, 18(3), 519–527.

Williams, Tom (2012). Review Exit, Pursued by a Bear. *Chicago Critic*. https://chicagocritic.com/exit-pursued-by-a-bear/.

  (2017). Review of Emilie: La Marquise Du Châtelet Defends Her Life Tonight. *Chicago Critic*. https://chicagocritic.com/emilie-la-marquise-du-chatelet-defends-her-life-tonight/.

Willis, Barry (2023). ASR Theater – Incomplete History Lesson: 'Justice: A New Musical' at MTC. Aisle Seat Review. 23 February. https://aisleseatreview.com/asr-theater-incomplete-history-lesson-justice-a-new-musical-at-mtc/.

Wolf, Stacy (2011). *Changed for Good. A Feminist History of the Broadway Musical*. Oxford: Oxford University Press.

  (2018). Gender and Sexuality. In Knapp, Raymond and Wolf, Stacy, eds., *Identities and Audiences in the Musical. Oxford Handbook of the American Musical*, vol 3. Oxford: Oxford University Press, pp. 33–58.

Wood, Alexander (2018). Review I and You (Hampstead Theatre). What's On Stage. 25 October. www.whatsonstage.com/news/review-i-and-you-hampstead-theatre_47886/.

Wren, Celia (2019). Dramatist Inserts Science in the Spotlight. *Washington Post*. 12 December 2019.

Acknowledgments

This research was enabled by a fellowship from the Spanish Ministry of Universities (Plan de Recuperación, Transformación y Resiliencia) and the Universidad Autónoma de Madrid (CA2/RSUE/2021–00383), which allowed me to be a Visiting Researcher at the Drama Department at Trinity College Dublin, University of Dublin (Ireland) for twelve months. Without the support of these three institutions, this Element would not have been possible. Special thanks to the staff, colleagues, and students at Trinity College Dublin who welcomed me, and provided me with an academic home away from home. Section 3, devoted to the intersection of Gunderson's theatre and the Medical Humanities, has been possible thanks to the fundings of the Research Project 'Gender and Pathography from a Transnational Perspective' (Spanish Ministry of Science and Innovation, PID2020-113330-GBI00).

It has been a privilege to write this Element and only made possible due to the generosity of Lauren Gunderson. Despite her busy professional life, she has always found the time to answer my questions, share her manuscripts, and even film herself talking about Shakespeare. I am very grateful for your support and impressed by your endless energy. Thanks as well to all the theatres that stage Gunderson's plays, and especially to those which have shared their photos and allowed their reproduction here: Echo Theatre and Cincinnati Playhouse in the Park.

Special thanks to all at Cambridge University Press, especially to Emily Hockley for your insightful early comments, to Julia Ford, and to Melissa Sihra and Elaine Aston, Series Editors, who supported, encouraged, and guided me so that this Element could materialise. Thank you for believing in this project from the start.

For their constant support and encouragement, I am grateful to my family and friends. I would like to thank Basia Ozieblo for inspiring conversations on feminism and theatre, and for providing very helpful feedback on early drafts. This Element would not have been possible without my son, Alonso, and my daughter, Olivia. The love and joy you bring to my life every day nurture my research and writing.

This Element is dedicated to Liv and Hugh Gibbons, our Dublin family by serendipity. I will always remain grateful to you beyond words.

Cambridge Elements

Women Theatre Makers

Elaine Aston
Lancaster University

Elaine Aston is internationally acclaimed for her feminism and theatre research. Her monographs include *Caryl Churchill* (1997); *Feminism and Theatre* (1995); *Feminist Theatre Practice* (1999); *Feminist Views on the English Stage* (2003); and *Restaging Feminisms* (2020). She has served as Senior Editor of Theatre Research International (2010–12) and President of the International Federation for Theatre Research (2019–23).

Melissa Sihra
Trinity College Dublin

Melissa Sihra is Associate Professor in Drama and Theatre Studies at Trinity College Dublin. She is author of *Marina Carr: Pastures of the Unknown* (2018) and editor of *Women in Irish Drama: A Century of Authorship and Representation* (2007). She was President of the Irish Society for Theatre Research (2011–15) and is currently researching a feminist historiography of the Irish playwright and co-founder of the Abbey Theatre, Lady Augusta Gregory.

Advisory Board

Nobuko Anan, *Kansai University, Japan*
Awo Mana Asiedu, *University of Ghana*
Ana Bernstein, *UNIRIO, Brazil*
Elin Diamond, *Rutgers, USA*
Bishnupriya Dutt, *JNU, India*
Penny Farfan, *University of Calgary, Canada*
Lesley Ferris, *Ohio State University, USA*
Lisa FitzPatrick, *University of Ulster, Northern Ireland*
Lynette Goddard, *Royal Holloway, University of London, UK*
Sarah Gorman, *Roehampton University, UK*
Aoife Monks, *Queen Mary, London University, UK*
Kim Solga, *Western University, Canada*
Denise Varney, *University of Melbourne, Australia*

About the Series

This innovative, inclusive series showcases women-identifying theatre makers from around the world. Expansive in chronological and geographical scope, the series encompasses practitioners from the late nineteenth century onwards and addresses a global, comprehensive range of creatives – from playwrights and performers to directors and designers.

Cambridge Elements

Women Theatre Makers

Elements in the Series

Maya Rao and Indian Feminist Theatre
Bishnupriya Dutt

Xin Fengxia and the Transformation of China's Ping Opera
Siyuan Liu

Emma Rice's Feminist Acts of Love
Lisa Peck

Women Making Shakespeare in the Twenty-First Century
Kim Solga

Clean Break Theatre Company
Caoimhe McAvinchey, Sarah Bartley, Deborah Dean and Anne-marie Greene

#WakingTheFeminists and the Data-Driven Revolution in Irish Theatre
Claire Keogh

The Theatre of Louise Lowe
Miriam Haughton

Ellen Terry, Shakespeare, and Suffrage in Australia and New Zealand
Kate Flaherty

Performing Female Intimacy in Japan's Takarazuka Revue
Nobuko Anan

Feminist Imagining in Polish and Ukrainian Theatres
Ewa Bal, Kasia Lech

Caryl Churchill's Eco-Socialist Feminism
Elaine Aston

Lauren Gunderson and Feminist Theatre in the Twenty-First Century
Noelia Hernando-Real

A full series listing is available at: www.cambridge.org/EWTM

For EU product safety concerns, contact us at Calle de José Abascal, 56–1°,
28003 Madrid, Spain or eugpsr@cambridge.org.

www.ingramcontent.com/pod-product-compliance
Lightning Source LLC
LaVergne TN
LVHW011854060526
838200LV00054B/4321